Bardic Deadlines

POETS ON POETRY

David Lehman, General Editor
Donald Hall, Founding Editor

New titles

John Hollander, *The Poetry of Everyday Life*
Geoffrey O'Brien, *Bardic Deadlines*

Recently published

Josephine Jacobsen, *The Instant of Knowing*
William Logan, *All the Rage*
Charles Simic, *Orphan Factory*
William Stafford, *Crossing Unmarked Snow*
Anne Stevenson, *Between the Iceberg and the Ship*
May Swenson, *Made with Words*
C. K. Williams, *Poetry and Consciousness*

Also available are collections by

A. R. Ammons, Robert Bly, Philip Booth, Marianne Boruch, Hayden Carruth, Fred Chappell, Amy Clampitt, Tom Clark, Douglas Crase, Robert Creeley, Donald Davie, Peter Davison, Tess Gallagher, Suzanne Gardinier, Allen Grossman, Thom Gunn, John Haines, Donald Hall, Joy Harjo, Robert Hayden, Daniel Hoffman, Jonathan Holden, Andrew Hudgins, Weldon Kees, Galway Kinnell, Mary Kinzie, Kenneth Koch, Richard Kostelanetz, Maxine Kumin, Martin Lammon (editor), David Lehman, Philip Levine, John Logan, William Matthews, William Meredith, Jane Miller, Carol Muske, John Frederick Nims, Gregory Orr, Alicia Ostriker, Marge Piercy, Anne Sexton, Charles Simic, Louis Simpson, William Stafford, Richard Tillinghast, Diane Wakoski, Alan Williamson, Charles Wright, and James Wright

Geoffrey O'Brien

Bardic Deadlines

REVIEWING POETRY, 1984–95

Ann Arbor

THE UNIVERSITY OF MICHIGAN PRESS

Published in the United States of America by
The University of Michigan Press
Manufactured in the United States of America
♾ Printed on acid-free paper

2001 2000 1999 1998 4 3 2 1

A CIP catalog record for this book is available from the British Library.

Library of Congress Cataloging-in-Publication Data

O'Brien, Geoffrey, 1948–
Bardic deadlines : reviewing poetry, 1984–95 / Geoffrey O'Brien.
p. cm. — (Poets on poetry)
ISBN 0-472-09683-4 (acid-free paper)
ISBN 0-472-06683-8 (pbk. : acid-free paper)
1. American poetry—History and criticism. 2. English poetry—History and criticism. I. Title. II. Series.
PS305 .027 1999
811.009—ddc21
98-25510
CIP

This book is dedicated
to the memory of my mother,
Margaret O'Brien
(1916–97)

Preface

All but two of the essays in this volume were written originally for the *Village Voice* and its (then-monthly) literary supplement, *VLS,* under the editorship of M. Mark. From the beginning M. encouraged me to go as far afield as I wished in reviewing poetry or anything else; it was part of her vision of the paper as a means to open up literary discussion beyond a slim shelf of A-list trade books and a select handful of scholarly titles, to bring in everything from specialized monographs and self-published chapbooks to 'zines and pulp novels, and to write about them without condescension and without resorting to the private jargon of the insider. The result was a publication in which it seemed natural to juxtapose ancient and contemporary, Kalidasa and Clark Coolidge, Emily Brontë and Miyazawa Kenji.

Had I been writing for a poetry magazine whose readers could be assumed (however unrealistically) to have some a priori interest in such writers, the tone might have been different. In the event I found it incomparably stimulating to start essentially from scratch, presuming as little as possible about what the reader was bringing to the piece. The only condition was that the writing must have interest as story or statement, quite independently of whether the reader was actually going to read the work under review. In the end it seemed a more bracing exercise than communing with the happy and hermetic few.

The essays included here owe a great deal to the editors with whom I worked at *VLS;* to M. Mark above all, and also to Polly Shulman, Tonice Sgrignoli, Walter Kendrick, and many others over the years. At the *New York Review of Books,* where two of these pieces were first published, I am indebted to the valuable guidance provided always by Robert Silvers and Barbara Epstein. For their encouragement and advice on the present volume, I am particularly grateful to David Lehman, Star Black, Joseph Donahue, and Robert Fagan. A number of pieces have been slightly revised and sometimes slightly compressed, although I have in general resisted the urge to amplify or update the views originally expressed.

Contents

Banging against the Edge of Language

For a fleeting moment in the late 1960s, American poetry bubbled with new possibilities. Various tendencies—Beats and Black Mountain poets, the newly rediscovered Objectivists (Zukofsky, Oppen, Reznikoff), a renaissance of black poets, an infusion of ethnopoetic traditions—appeared to be blending, in typical sixties fashion, into a cosmic synthesis. Perhaps the key element in this euphoria was a new awareness of poetry as oral performance. The academic tradition, with its emphasis on rational analysis of a printed text, would be supplanted by the ecstatic presence of the Living Word. The poet as shaman would once again hold the tribe spellbound with a visionary chant.

This surge of energy led to a proliferation of poetic activity beyond anyone's expectations. Throughout the 1970s, chapbooks, magazines, readings, poet-in-residence programs abounded, often with the help of government arts funding. Yet by the end of the decade many poets were thoroughly depressed, not merely by the enormous amount of slipshod writing that resulted, but by the increasing insularity of poetry itself. The rise of a "poetry bureaucracy" focused on grant allocations and academic sinecures only emphasized that the mass audiences of the sixties had faded, leaving an ever-growing number of poets and poetasters thrashing about in

Review of *The L=A=N=G=U=A=G=E Book* edited by Bruce Andrews and Charles Bernstein (Carbondale: Southern Illinois University Press, 1984), *Resistance* by Charles Bernstein (Windsor, VT: Awede, 1983), *ABC* by Ron Silliman (Berkeley, CA: Tuumba, 1983), and *Defenestration of Prague* by Susan Howe (New York: Kulchur Foundation, 1983). Reprinted from *VLS,* April 1984.

competition for the remaining readers and listeners. It began to appear that without arts funding and university support, there would be little space for poetry. More fundamentally, poets had a sense of staleness, of old aesthetic gestures repeated out of habit, old strategies applied to a radically altered situation.

In the midst of this lassitude, one group of writers managed to stir thing up. Centered in San Francisco and New York, published by magazines like *This, Roof,* and *Hills,* and by Lyn Hejinian's Tuumba Press, they were quickly perceived as that longed-for phenomenon, a New Movement. Variously dubbed "nonreferential," "language-centered," or simply "language" poets, the group has grown to the point where Ron Silliman, in a recent survey, lists eighty-nine poets. As most of them are quite prolific, we're talking about hundreds of books, a corpus produced in a single decade and already difficult to keep track of.

Language writing—to adopt the conventional but unfortunate label for writing that is "not about anything," that dismantles grammar and uses words as detached objects, confronting the reader with an "unreadable" text—invented few of its techniques. Avant-gardists from Stein to Joyce to the Concretists had already explored most ways of distorting and rearranging language. The tone, however, was different: instead of bohemian exuberance, these efforts to short-circuit aesthetic responses had a deliberate, almost plodding seriousness. *L=A=N=G=U=A=G=E,* the movement's leading theoretical journal, made clear that the poets' disruptive language practices (to use their own favorite term) sprang above all from an analysis of the social role of language. Charles Bernstein, Bruce Andrews, Ron Silliman, and others wrote essays inquiring into the relations between poetry and politics. They saw political poetry not as a matter of affixing slogans to conventional lyrics, in order to sell the Revolution with heartrending images, but rather of focusing on the oppressive structures of grammar, syntax, and vocabulary. At the same time, pieces like "The Political Economy of Poetry" and "The Dollar Value of Poetry" explored in concrete terms the social position of poets in America.

The L=A=N=G=U=A=G=E Book, which comprises a major chunk of the material that appeared in the magazine between

1978 and 1982, is an essential source. With its blend of voices and crisscrossing dialogues, the book has an almost novelistic density. It is also a rather overpowering dose when taken at once, especially given the predilection of many contributors for words like *anoegenetic, syntagm,* and *margination.* Even writers decrying the tyranny of abstract nouns display an inordinate fondness for them.

Yet through these terminological thickets runs a persistent theme: in capitalist society language tends, like everything else, to turn into a commodity. In keeping with the aesthetic dictates of bourgeois representationalism, it serves as a transparent medium; the reader loses sight of the words as things in themselves and perceives only the socially defined "reality" they encode. In this way, society represses the process by which meaning is produced. The language writer deconstructs the meaning-creating mechanisms of language. The result is an opaque text in which, as Bruce Andrews puts it, "reading becomes the first *production,* rather than consumption—not a relay of an author's vain transcription of a representational content. Reading *operates* the text, is a rewriting, a new inscription." In this context, the language poet-theorists make much of Barthes's distinction between the "writerly" and the "readerly." Rather than aiming for the "hypnosis" and commodity fetishism encouraged by descriptive writing, the text embodies "an esthetics of fragmentation and discontinuity" (Nick Piombino) because "all notions of form are implicitly coercive" (Ray DiPalma). Language constructs thought; it is forced into rigidifying structures to control thought; only by splitting apart language can new thoughts emerge: "Where once one sought a vocabulary for ideas, now one seeks ideas for vocabularies" (Lyn Hejinian).

Development of active reading, in contrast with the passive acceptance instilled by "a denying and repressive order" (Bruce Andrews), is an essential strategy in this effort to break the spell of standard language. It is also a way of coping with poetry's central malaise—the lack of an audience—by building that audience as part of its process. Study group replaces packed auditorium as operating model.

All this is, among other things, a response to the bloated vagueness of much poetic posturing in the sixties and since. The process of deconstructing breaks a diffuse cloud of warm feeling into its component signifiers. As Charles Bernstein remarks, "The cant of 'make it personal' & 'let it flow' are avoidances—by mystification—of some very compelling problems that swirl around truthtelling, confession, bad faith, false self, authenticity, faith, etc." If the previously dominant image of populist bard reflected an ego caught up in delusions of grandeur, these poets take apart the notion of personal identity and offer an authorless text.

They seek literature as critique, literature as negation of the ruling discourse, literature that can "undermine the historic confidence of the bourgeoisie" (Ron Silliman) by disconnecting signifier and signified. This is not the place to look for a world of depth and balanced proportions. Depthlessness is precisely what's intended: the page as an exposed presence, with nothing hidden. Indeed, the effect of much language poetry is of a flat chaos, a bare surface flecked with remnants of what once were meanings. We might take this as a poetry for the era of lowered expectations. You wanted song, vision, prophecy perhaps? Sorry, the factory isn't making them anymore. We can, however, show you how you conceived your wants in the first place.

There is a contradiction at the core of these essays: the desire to do away with the claustrophobic structures of language is at odds with a relentlessly intellectual approach that thrives on those very structures. As poetic schools go, this one draws from philosophy and political science far more than belles lettres. The book pays passing homage to Gertrude Stein and Louis Zukofsky, but more frequently refers us to the likes of Barthes, Derrida, Lacan, Deleuze, Kristeva, Klossowski, Foucault, Debord—in short, the whole francophone panoply of "Freudo-Marxism."

Philosophical explanation can say a great deal about poetry, but it cannot do poetry's work. While philosophy longs for a pure intellect free of contingency, poetry is hopelessly mired in the contingent and impure. It is grounded in the specific rather than the categorical; it speaks from the viscera as well as the critical mind. In poetry, finally, it's the lines that count, without alibis or second guessing. Citation and theory are no substitute for cadence and vitality.

Another pitfall of this philosophical approach is thinking

in terms of neat oppositions: transparency/opacity, readerly/writerly, closed text/opened text. Various proposed enemies—capitalist commodity-consciousness, representationalism, linguistic referentiality—fuse into a simplified Them from which We will be delivered by "the larger struggle against all forms of preconditioning" (Steve McCaffery). This reductionism evades other possibilities, such as a poetic art that joins transparency and opacity, so that we "see the picture" while clearly perceiving the elements of the illusion.

Meanwhile, what of the poems themselves? Probably more people will ransack *The L=A=N=G=U=A=G=E Book* for the promised "new ideas," reveling in the abstractly imagined pleasures of "text production," than will seek out the work that inspired the cogitation. Expository prose encourages a restless anxiety to look for the shortest path to "the point," even if the point is that there is no point. Poetry, on the other hand, asks to be lived with a while. It's a commitment.

There's always a difference between talk about poetry and the work itself. I doubt that the unprepared reader of Charles Bernstein's *Resistance* would deduce the coolly logical terms in which he had defined his poetics. (For that matter, to many readers Bernstein might not seem any more obscure than "normal" poetry.) Taken in patches, the words seem truly drained of meaning—"clip mimic dazed proclivity almonds"—but the overall cadence sustains a lyric structure that imparts the "feel" of emotion without tying it to a familiar gesture. Bernstein toys with the possibility of ordinary statement; at moments his purposefully opaque lines give way to language we can almost hear without the double take of incomprehension: "Time is the grainy thing that cordons / its own descent like lips / drawn to a fire."

Although such lines are finally no more "meaningful" than the rest, temperament survives deconstruction. A vocabulary of erosion and loss—in "Stunment" we have "sputter," "curdled," "somberer," "no more," "wear away," "displaced," "outworn" within a dozen lines—asserts itself in the absence of graspable syntactic connections. The reader—at any rate this reader—finds himself willy-nilly asking the impossible questions. "What sort of a fellow is he? What kind of day was it? How did he feel about what was going on?" From the answers I invent, I create my "impression of the poem." This primacy of the reader is presumably what Bernstein intended, though I don't know how happy he would be with what my mind has done to his text.

Ron Silliman's *ABC* represents the first three sections of a long "new prose" work in progress called *The Alphabet,* evidently a summing up of some kind. In Bernstein's poems we are inside a mind continually banging against the edges of language; Silliman wants to place consciousness in the world, to lay the words alongside the other objects. His materiality fits in with his political intentions, an insistence on the "hard facts" of what is out there. From the first section, "Albany":

> My father withheld child support, forcing my mother to live with her parents, my brother and I to be raised together in a small room. Grandfather called them niggers. I can't afford an automobile. Far across the calm bay stood a complex of long yellow buildings, a prison.

By the time we get to "Carbon," it's the mind's puns and misleading echoes that are under observation: "But this is a false tart . . . alcohol is its own remark . . . Coming soon to a paragraph near you." The point is not to display Silliman's wit but to expose the mechanisms of thinking. The tension in *ABC* is between thoughts going their own way and the intentionality of political consciousness. Silliman's strength is his capacity for sustained attention to gradually shifting mental patterns; he asks, however, for unlimited patience on the part of the reader. Such are the trade-offs.

Of all the books under discussion here, Susan Howe's *Defenestration of Prague* excites me most. Again temperament proves decisive; Howe's fragmentation and discontinuity are quite different from anyone else's. While Bernstein's words seem to hover near meaning in a state of frustrated desire and Silliman's resemble a rough-textured collage of disparate found objects, Howe's words give the impression of echoing another, hidden poetry of which we catch only fragments, like an opera sung in another room—except the other room is death, or history, or the ineffable. Her vocabulary includes the whole past of language. The words are like magnetic filings that adhere uncertainly to a receding body of meaning. Bits crumble into gnomic phrases—"nimble multiplying spirit" or "Search for the dead" or "Unseen waters of the word"—and Howe strings them into haunting tunes, as in the long poem sequence "Speeches at the Barriers":

> Clear night
> Cassiopeia—
>
> To the glass house by water
>
> hurried elf
> and bedlam beggar
>
> lonely hellward nursery tale manner
>
> Know buried cities
> Know the combustible dark

In *Defenestration* and in her 1982 book *Pythagorean Silence,* Howe risks plunging into the most played-out area of language, the realm of the "profound" words. I don't know another poet capable of using the words "passion," "truth," "glory," and "beauty" in four lines and getting them to say something new. Her ear is uncanny, but it's what she's listening for in the first place that makes the difference.

The presence of the past is overwhelming in Howe's work—as it is in our lives—but in the spaces between her words I hear an opening to the future. While she locates the deepest mysteries within rather than beyond language, Howe's work acknowledges that the need for visionary poetry persists even in the absence of belief. The more rigorous practitioners of language poetry make no such acknowledgment and their work pays a price in diminished emotional impact; ultimately, readers ask more than a demonstration of language's insufficiencies.

Destination Unknown

Gustaf Sobin

Although Gustaf Sobin has lived for twenty years in southern France, the fact is not immediately obvious from his poetry. He isn't, in other words, another American proponent of what Kenneth Koch once called the Fulbright School of Verse, for whom Europe serves as an open-air boutique well stocked with literary allusions, picturesque anecdotes, and only the most tasteful shades of landscape coloring. Except for an occasional olive tree or rose window, Sobin might be guiding us through a remote corner of Tibet:

> that overhanging
> jelly-
> headed light. where path
> would turn into pine, and pine into those
> flaccid, ice-
> green
> fires.

Sobin is a landscape artist whose terrain is language, that frustrating and unstable middle ground which tries to mediate internal and external realities. His single-minded purpose is to unite what's outside (the almond flowers, the rocks, "the seed- / beaded tops of the / grasses") and what's inside (the syllables of the poem, the flow of breath) into a seamless speech that neither declares nor describes but "by which all things, unto them-

---

Review of *The Earth as Air* by Gustaf Sobin (New York: New Directions, 1984). Reprinted from *VLS,* June 1984.

selves, are rendered. by which, by uttering, we *are*." He wants "a taut, vibratory weave," "a luminous tapestry of sound" in which we send "our syllables . . . over and over, instead of ourselves, *past* ourselves, as if sacrificial."

It's a heady enterprise, this desperate leaping at the barrier that separates language from the world, this effort to make "the created, at last, syncretic with creation." In common poetic usage one is supposed to approach such things delicately, aiming at understated, almost imperceptible epiphanies. Here, on the contrary, there is no buildup, no setting of the stage; we are midflight from page one. Rather than developing toward a neat point, the poems sustain a trancelike steady state; they do not so much end as break off. Sobin makes no concessions to the colloquial mannerisms of contemporary verse: he's after a linguistic equivalent to exaltation, and his characteristic mode might be termed lyrical-obsessive. In this kind of writing, if you look down you're dead.

He approvingly quotes Mallarmé's "Everything I've created has been by elimination," but Sobin's minimalism is *profuse.* No matter how abstract their narrative order or descriptive detail, these poems seem nearly Swinburnian in their pursuit of the gorgeous:

> wild buds on their wind-
> ballasted antlers, beast struck,
> its love belling dumbly in the rain-
> darkened rose.

It's a poetry steered by the melodic and tactile qualities of the words, as if (reversing Pope) the sense were an echo to the sound. The syllables are like an advance guard hollowing out the space in which perception can take place. The poem forms itself word by word, inching forward without preconceived argument, its destination unknown:

> ploughed
> ice, where an
> eye

swims, scarce
muscle, up
over

its
clotted ditch

The physicality that Sobin brings to poetry is not that of inert chunks of words on a page, but of organic matter in motion. Even though (as he remarks in the ars poetica that closes the book) language carries within itself the vapor "of death itself," poetry's curious task is to transmute that into "a death continuously discharged, expelled, projected . . . a death *kept alive.*" The point would be merely rhetorical if Sobin did not deliver the authentic hum of transmission, a real-time map of energy pulsing from instant to instant. However elusive the philosophical underpinnings, the robust palpability of their workmanship makes these poems as pleasurable as any I've read in years. Their rhythmic vitality demonstrates again that before words can be emotionally moving, they have to *move.*

The Last Medieval Poet

John Clare

In the early nineteenth century, in the fen country of Northamptonshire, a largely self-educated field hand began composing poems. Sometimes he worked on them in his head while he labored, memorizing the long strings of verses until he had a chance to transcribe them; sometimes, as he recounts in a fragmentary autobiography, "I used to drop down behind a hedge bush or dyke & write down my things upon the crown of my hat. . . . thus I went on writing my thoughts down & correcting them at leisure spending my Sundays in the woods or heaths to be alone for that purpose." Most of these poems recapitulated the surroundings in which they were written: "I hunted curious flowers in rapture & muttered thoughts in their praise I lovd the pasture with its rushes & thistles & sheep tracks I adored the wild marshy fen with its solitary hernshaw sweeing along in its melancholy sky." He was astonishingly prolific, writing as many as eight poems a day, and acknowledging that "when I am in the fit I write as much in one week as would knock ye up a fair size vol."

His neighbors, unaware of this secret vocation, classed him as an odd and idle fellow given mainly to drinking ale and consorting with gypsies in the forest, when not wandering around talking to himself in apparent distraction. He did odd jobs, hiring himself out as a tavern worker or a gardener, and all in all was not a desirable prospect; he loved (with what turned out to be an enduring passion) a prosperous farmer's daughter, Mary Joyce, "but when she grew to womanhood she felt her station above mine at least I felt that she thought so." Even in the

---

Reprinted from *VLS,* February 1985.

context of an impoverished village, he floundered near the bottom of the social heap.

A series of lucky chances (or, as he came to feel, perhaps not so lucky) reversed his fortunes. When he set about in rather naive fashion to find an outlet for his verses, he could hardly have foreseen that his manuscripts would be taken up by a leading London publisher, whose list already included Hazlitt, Lamb, and Keats. The poet's image as an untutored rustic paid off; his first book, *Poems Descriptive of Rural Life and Scenery* (1820) was a surprise hit, going through four editions in a single year. The twenty-seven-year-old peasant bard made his first trip to London to find himself a celebrity: "on the night that we got into London it was announced in the play Bills that a song of mine was to be sung at Covent Garden by Madame Vestris." Wealth and lasting fame appeared to be at hand.

He didn't know that he had already peaked. The following year a second book, *The Village Minstrel,* attracted good initial sales but then plummeted. Its delayed successor, *The Shepherd's Calendar,* abridged and bowdlerized by an increasingly reluctant publisher, sold hardly at all. The fad was over. The poet landed back where he had started, living in poverty with an illiterate wife and seven children he could barely support. He worked in the fields again, drank heavily, fell prey to agitation and depression, all the while continuing to write and firmly believing that a literary comeback was imminent. In 1830 he leaped onstage during a local production of *The Merchant of Venice* and assaulted the actor playing Shylock. Five years later he applied for medical treatment: "I am very unwell. . . . sounds affect me very much & things evil as well as good thoughts are continually rising in my mind I cannot sleep for I am asleep as it were with my eyes open & feel chills come over me & a great sort of night mare awake." In 1837 he was removed to an experimental (and surprisingly humane) asylum in Epping Forest.

Of the many obsessions and delusions that by now afflicted him, none was more intense than the fixation on his lost love Mary Joyce. He became convinced that he had married her, and to her he dedicated the poetry that continued to flow from him. Escaping from Epping Forest, he walked more than eighty miles from Essex to Northamptonshire unfed and unsheltered—"I satisfied my hunger by eating the grass by the road side which seemed to taste something like bread"—in a vain search for a woman who had died several years earlier: "Mary was not there neither could I get any information about her further than the old story of her being dead six years ago. . . . but I took no notice of the blarney having seen her myself about a twelvemonth ago alive and well and as young as ever."

For a few months his wife tried to care for him at home, but when his behavior turned violent he was again committed, this time to the public institution at Northampton, where he remained for the last twenty-two years of his life. He never stopped writing: in the first complete edition of his late work published by Oxford, the Northampton poems fill some eight hundred pages.

Such, in brief, was the wretched life of John Clare, of which a fuller account can be found in Edward Storey's excellent biography, *A Right to Song*. For those who like their poets mad, Clare seems to offer an ultimate instance of inspired lunacy. Certainly his contemporaries thought so; the doctors who committed him to Northampton Asylum cited as a precipitating factor in his illness "years addicted to poetical prosings," and toward the end of his life Clare himself stated: "Literature has destroyed my head and brought me here." Yet a look at the full range of his work shows that Clare is far from being a figure of Romantic isolation. Quite the contrary: this preeminently sane poet sets forth a healing vision of interrelation without parallel in European poetry. As many readers continue to discover, his work adds up to a kind of ecological epic, where every twig and snail and linnet is part and product of a seamless organic whole.

Decades have passed since Robert Graves and Geoffrey Grigson praised him and Benjamin Britten set his lines to music, yet Clare is only now being integrated into the academic canon of English literature. It has taken 120 years to begin publishing a definitive edition of his works. As if it weren't enough for Clare to have been overwhelmed with obstacles in his lifetime, even after his death his work has had to struggle to find its place. Whatever made Clare an outsider continues to keep his poetry separate from the mainstream, quarantined as a "special case" when we should receive it as essential communication. What

Clare has to say couldn't be more urgent: in singing of a way of life where humans can exist harmoniously with animals and plants, and of that life's destruction in the name of progress, he sings the loss of our planet. Rooted in nature as he was, he anticipated all the more vividly the death of what he loved most. Already we find it hard to retrieve the consciousness from which he wrote: most of us will never feel that close to our soil again.

Although born in the Age of Enlightenment, Clare speaks in the tones of a more archaic culture. Much of the daily life he knew as a child would not have been out of place in a medieval Book of Hours. The men still labored on behalf of the lord of the manor, plowing fields not yet enclosed, sharing the use of common lands according to patterns unchanged since the thirteenth century. The natural world penetrated existence too thoroughly to be conceived of as other. So it isn't surprising if in the scurryings of Clare's birds and beasts we hear the cadences of the last medieval poet:

> From dark green clumps among the dripping grain
> The lark with sudden impulse starts and sings
> And mid the smoaking rain
> Quivers her russet wings.

It was also a handmade, homemade culture in which, as the preeminent Clare scholar Eric Robinson notes, "people's amusement was made by them and not for them." Clare modeled his verse technique on poets like Cowper and Thomson, but the deeper sources of his writing lie in the traditions he was born to: May festivals, sheepshearings, ballads and reels (he was an accomplished fiddler), morris dances, fireside tales. He speaks of "weeding wheat in the spring with old women listening to their songs & stories," and recalls that his first reading consisted of "6 penny pamphlets that are in the possession of every doorcalling hawker & found on every bookstall at fairs & markets. . . . *Little Red Riding Hood, Valentine & Orson, Jack & the Giant, Long Tom the Carrier.*. . . . they were the whole world of literature to me & I knew of no other."

The chief factor militating against full literary acceptance of Clare has always been his educational shortcomings: not just the errors and idiosyncrasies of his grammar and spelling or the homeliness of his meters, but above all his lack of grounding in intellectual discourse, and the consequent alleged poverty of his ideas. By this argument the preponderance of raw perception in Clare's poetry stems from his inability to *do* anything with what his five senses were so vigorously taking in. Clare's own editors and upper-class patrons perpetually counseled him to ease up on things and creatures and instead cultivate sentiments and morals.

The poetry Clare was inventing evokes parallels both ancient (the verbal scroll paintings of Wang Wei and T'ao Ch'ien) and modern (William Carlos Williams's "no ideas but in things"), but his immediate contemporaries were unprepared for it. No one else in the nineteenth century hews so closely to the physical object: for Clare, the "short shrubby bushes nibbl'd by the sheep" or "the warped and punished trunk of stunted oak" are sufficient to themselves. Paradise is identical with the most ordinary and minute particulars: "I feel so calm I seem to find / A world I never felt before / A heaven fills my clouded mind. . . . / And yet they are but common things / Green hedges bowering oer the grass / And one old tree that stoops and flings / Its boughs oer water smooth as glass."

In the ninth Duino Elegy, Rilke asks: "Are we, perhaps, here just for saying: House, Bridge, Fountain, Gate, Jug, Olive Tree, Window?" Clare is the rare poet who does precisely that. He creates things by naming them, and so in his poems we have the sense not of reading a description but of inhabiting a world. He practices the most primitive kind of imitative magic, reconstructing nature in language so that he can fulfill his profound desire to immerse himself in it. He wants to capture not just the isolated image, the specimen neatly pinned to the wall for relaxed contemplation, but a coiling and intermingling continuum. He summons up a world of speed, surprise, sudden emergences, crossing paths, a polyrhythmic reverberation of natural noises:

> from mossy barn the owl
> Bobs hasty out—wheels round and scared as soon
> As hastily retires—the ducks grow wild

And from the muddy pond fly up and wheel
A circle round the village and soon tired
Plunge in the pond again—the maids in haste
Snatch from the orchard hedge the mizled cloaths
And laughing hurry in to keep them dry.

Clare's celebration of a rural Eden preserves a pre-Christian undercurrent of European tradition, an animist worship of generative powers. The Sunday bells reach him remotely across an expanse of heath. He seeks more ancient shrines, like the bush where a nightingale sings "lost in a wilderness of listening leaves" or the spot where "pilewort blazes round the hill / Beside the sleeping lamb." He is always moving toward recesses, interiors, imperceptible hiding places, attempting if only in memory "To trace the path of briar entangled holt / Or bushy closen where the wanton colt / Crops the young juicey leaves from off the hedge." Identifying himself with insect or bird, he finds the immense spaces concealed within thickets or hollow trees.

His style wasn't achieved in a single intuitive leap. The earliest poem included in the Oxford Authors collection of his work echoes the stately bombast of many a late Augustan ode:

Hail humble Helpstone where thy valies spread
And thy mean village lifts its lowly head
Unknown to grandeur and unknown to fame
No minstrel boasting to advance thy name
Unlettered spot unheard in poets song
Where bustling labour drives the hours along

In the poetic models available to Clare, landscape was orderly, its rectangular lines as symmetrical as the parallelisms of a rhymed couplet. Nature had its hierarchies, with mountains judged superior to badgers' dens, and men more significant than nuthatches or earthworms. It was an aesthetic predisposed to neatly framed vistas in the manner of Claude Lorrain's paintings. Timothy Brownlow, in his brilliantly free-ranging *John Clare and Picturesque Landscape,* recalls the popular device known as a Claude glass, "a tinted convex mirror often carried by tourists and artists, which gave the landscape the ideal qualities of a Claude painting." Such static, soft-focus pictorialism, reducing nature to a posed cluster of tame abstractions, came with the literary territory Clare inherited. It took his radical simplicity to break through that artificiality by shaping the way he wrote to what he saw, rather than the other way around.

He accomplished his quiet revolution not by changing the forms in which he wrote—his meters and rhyme schemes remained simple and old-fashioned to the end—but by transforming them from inside. Within his outwardly well ordered formats a new kind of poem takes shape, a poem with no fixed point of arrival or departure, which explores the interior of a landscape from a constantly shifting viewpoint: "open field composition" in the most literal sense. Where earlier poets gave the standard tour of the property, Clare stumbles on unexpected wildflowers and hidden nests. We can move through his poems as if walking at liberty through actual places, luxuriating in the absence of a rhetorical superstructure to guide our steps.

The absence of that superstructure was Clare's great failing in the eyes of his contemporaries. Even Keats felt that "the Description too much prevailed over the Sentiment"—while Clare characteristically complained of Keats that "behind every rosebush he looks for a Venus & under every Laurel a thrumming Apollo." Clare's problem was that although he knew quite well what he was up to, a peasant poet was not supposed to be the best judge of what was good for him. His discoverer and self-appointed literary agent, Edward Drury, even withheld money from Clare on the grounds that he would be incapable of managing it, and cautioned that "if he is removed from his humble occupation of gardening his talent will be ruined." Regardless of their admiration for Clare's poetic genius, his advisers felt duty bound to treat him as a child.

Alternately coddled and reprimanded, Clare himself seesawed between rebellion and submission. Told that his grammar must be amended, he exploded: "grammar in learning is like tyranny in government—confound the bitch I'll never be her slave & have a vast good mind not to alter the verse in question." In the end, however, he had no choice. If his poems were to be published at all, they would appear with spelling and punctuation normalized, "ungrateful" political passages (such as a diatribe against wealth) deleted, frank sexual images glossed over, dialect names of flowers and animals transmuted into more refined equivalents. Many aspects of country life—its ruder smells and textures and noises—were deemed too jarring for polite sensibilities. Clare might continue to insist that "I heartily desire no word of mine to be altered," but he knew when he was beaten. Only in recent decades, due largely to the efforts of Eric Robinson and his collaborators, have the original versions of Clare's poems been restored from the surviving manuscripts.

Clare's first readers wanted to see him as a reassuring emblem of bucolic innocence, posed against an unchanging background of streams and meadows. They weren't prepared to grasp either the intensity of his ecstasies within his "paradise of poesy" or the correspondingly intense bitterness with which he witnessed the erosion of that Eden. In his primal vision the immediate presence of nature was itself eternity: "Cowslaps golden blooms / That in the closen and the meadow comes / Shall come when kings and empires fade and dye." Yet when he wrote that, his landscape had already altered beyond recognition. Enclosure—the cutting up and fencing off of fields in the name of agricultural efficiency—had by 1820 effectively eliminated the world of Clare's childhood. Propelled by a rapidly increasing rural population, enclosure and its accompanying deforestation wrought devastation on the wildlife that for Clare was the heart of the land.

The poet's attachment to the scenes he knew as a child went well beyond ordinary nostalgia. His response to the disappearance of a favorite bush or tree was lifelong inconsolable mourning. Some positivists have argued that his anguish at enclosure represented a neurotic response to a measure that in fact benefited the peasantry economically. But Clare, as usual, was not thinking only of people. The freedom whose loss he mourned—

> Fence now meets fence in owners little bounds
> Of field and meadow large as garden grounds
> In little parcels little minds to please
> With men and flocks imprisoned ill at ease

—was a freedom belonging to all life-forms. In "The Lament of Swordy Well" he speaks in the voice of a once-fertile stone quarry now mined into barrenness: "And me they turned me inside out / For sand and grit and stones / And turned my old green hills about / And pickt my very bones." The stripped ground can no longer sustain its rabbits and butterflies and clover; its "bees flye round in feeble rings / And find no blossom bye."

The crisis of his relation to nature coincided with the crisis of his writing. In 1832 a well-meaning patron, Earl Fitzwilliam, sought to relieve Clare's financial burdens by providing him with a cottage three miles from his native village. Although the distance was small, Clare's reaction to this uprooting was profound depression and a sense that "poesy is on the wane / I hardly know her face again." This supposed drying up of the creative impulse engendered some of his greatest poetry, in which his sadness at removal from his birthplace merges with a more general grief over the obliteration of the landscape itself. In a triumph of particularity, he gives universal resonance to the place names of an obscure village:

> By Langley bush I roam but the bush hath left its hill
> On cowper green I stray tis a desert strange and chill
> And spreading lea close oak ere decay had penned its will
> To the axe of the spoiler and self interest fell a prey
> And cross berry way and old round oaks narrow lane
> With its hollow trees like pulpits I shall never see again

The life-giving waters of childhood metamorphose into an image of desolation: "though the brook is running still / It runs a naked brook cold and chill."

The poems just preceding the final breakdown have a peculiar intensity: the poet seems to disappear altogether, losing himself in sharply focused images of hunted animals, like the badger who "starts and grins and drives the crowd agen / Till kicked and torn and beaten out he lies / And leaves his hold and cackles groans and dies." Clare's identity had become nearly impossible to maintain. An inhabitant of two worlds, he had been evicted from both: rejected by the literary world and increasingly shunned by his neighbors, of whom he had written,

"I live here among the ignorant like a lost man. . . . they hardly dare talk in my company for fear I should mention them in my writings." The contradictions involved in being a "peasant poet" put Clare in a special position—which turned out to be no position at all.

In his madness Clare embraced the nonidentity that had been thrust on him. The poet who had identified with everything found that everything had disappeared, leaving a bare disconnected self: "I feel I am, I only know I am." Severed from the locations that had given him his sense of reality, he writes of an unmoored landscape without coordinates—"Where stones will turn to flooding streams / Where plains will rise like ocean waves / Where life will fade like visioned dreams / And mountains darken into caves"—a landscape where he is condemned "At once to be, & not to be."

At their most intense, the asylum poems express with almost unendurable directness the internal geography of Clare's psychosis. The most striking is "Child Harold," an ambitious long poem (the title but little else stems from Clare's occasional delusion of being Byron) that attempts to resolve his obsession with the phantasmal Mary. Over a ground note of despair, Clare weaves eerily lovely landscapes that flicker briefly and subside:

> This twilight seems a veil of gause & mist
> Trees seem dark hills between the earth & sky
> Winds sob awake & then a gusty hist
> Fanns through the wheat like serpent gliding bye

But the poet's wandering in his dream forest are shot through with sudden emotional storms: "My soul is apathy—a ruin vast / Time cannot clear the ruined mass away / My life is hell." The poem, dating from 1841, feels like a final convulsive effort to break through the cloud descending on him. It fails because Clare cannot grasp that his symbol of life, Mary, is leading him into a living death: "How dull the glooms cover / This meadow & fen / Where I as a lover / Seek Mary agen." In all innocence his love poems turn into vampire poems.

After the removal to Northampton Asylum, Clare no longer struggles; he merely survives. The thousand pages of *The Later*

Poems (published in two volumes by Oxford University Press) settle into a curiously bland cheerfulness. Where his earlier poems were acts of discovery and exploration, the poems of his madness resemble holding actions. He keeps the demons at bay by writing lyric after lyric about an increasingly unreal rural paradise; the fields that were once present in the poem have become remote, attenuated memories. In place of the open, questing shape of the early work, we find the predictable patterns of the sentimental ballad: "And we will walk the meadow love / And we will walk the grove / And by the winding river love / We'll walk and talk of love / And by the white thorn bushes love / Just budding into green / Where the shaded fountain rushes love / We'll steal a kiss unseen."

Gone is the swarming population of drovers and woodcutters and gossiping alewives that once filled his lines. The world has been reduced to a cast of two, lover and a beloved just vanished or about to vanish. He takes refuge in a single stereotyped instant, playing it back over and over again: on a beautiful morning in spring a young maiden catches his eye as she walks across the meadow or steps over the stream. The botanical and zoological precision of his youth gives way to generalizations; he writes "bird" or "tree" where he would once not only have named it but shown us the color scheme of its feathers or the tracery of its leaves.

At times the painted backdrop shifts to reveal the emptiness underneath. Even the violets, emblems of rejuvenation, now "seem as sweet, yet valueless." The ultimate horror for Clare was to look at nature and feel no kinship: "The sun shines wan and pale / Chill blows the northern gale / And odd leaves shake and shiver on the tree / While I am left alone / Chilled as a mossy stone / And all the world is frowning over me." Once he had been like a lens shaped for perceiving the world, but now the glass was cracked, and he knew it: "as the winds the water stir / The mirrors change & flye." These moments of sudden self-awareness generated a dozen or so lyrics—such as "A Vision," "An Invite to Eternity," or "How hot the sun rushes"—as powerful in their concentrated simplicity as the songs of Blake.

The years of confinement were mostly tranquil, although interrupted by violent episodes. Clare was free (until the asylum's policy changed) to wander about in town, writing poems upon request for any passing stranger, a harmless and contemplative figure: "His favorite spot is under the All Saints Portico where he sits frequently for hours together." To outsiders he seemed utterly detached, lost in an uninterrupted reverie. "I told Clare I had been much pleased with his lines on the daisy," wrote one visitor. " 'Ugh it is a tidy little thing' replied he without raising his eyes or appearing in the slightest degree gratified by my praise." From the changing weather of the poems we learn that there were days of mental torture ("A bright grey eye or black it knocks mine through / & leaves them dim as stars fall'n from above / Electric shocks they come from God knows who") and days when his old vision was at least partially restored to him: "The pilewort glitters 'neath the pale blue sky / The little robin has its nest begun / And grass green linnets round the bushes fly."

In the end it was as if his objective eye turned inward in a kind of lyrical catatonia. The poetry that had been his escape was now his only dwelling place. In place of trees and flowers he inhabited a country of language. But for Clare poetry had always represented ultimate reality. The melody he had spent his life tracing was nothing less than an endless restatement of the creation of the world:

What is songs eternity
Come and see
Melodys of earth and sky
Here they be
Songs once sung to adams ears
Can it be
—Ballads of six thousand years
Thrive thrive
Songs awakened with the spheres
Alive

Poet Laureate of Matter

Hugh MacDiarmid

Listening to Hugh MacDiarmid read his poetry was like encountering an ancient bard, a Caedmon or Taliesin unaccountably flung up into the technological era. He was eighty-one when I heard him, but his voice—despite the cigarettes he chain-smoked throughout the reading—expanded vibrantly to fill the normally restrained precincts of the Poetry Society of London. For an hour or so he succeeded in making us forget that this was 1974, and that poetry had long since devolved into a hothouse blossom cultivated only in the most overrefined interiors of a listless civilization. By the time he launched into "On a Raised Beach," with its catalog of minerals—"Cream-coloured caen-stone, chatoyant pieces, / Celadon and corbeau, bistre and beige, / Glaucous, hoar, enfouldered, cyathiform"—and Norn invocations—"They hvarf from me in all directions / Over the hurdifell"—we were ready to believe ourselves cast with him on an uninhabited inlet of the North Sea, ready to begin everything all over again. He radiated such energy that the considerably younger man who introduced him seemed decrepit by comparison and in the question-and-answer session after the reading—so often an occasion for barely suppressed tedium—he leaped from subject to subject with obvious delight, tossing out jokes, political asides, brief penetrating comments on literary figures from Robert Burns to James Joyce. He was clearly ready to go on

---

Review of *The Complete Poems of Hugh MacDiarmid* edited by Michael Grieve and W. R. Aitken, rev. ed. (Harmondsworth: Penguin Books, 1985), and *The Letters of Hugh MacDiarmid* edited by Alan Bold (Athens: University of Georgia Press, 1985). Reprinted from *VLS,* May 1985.

all night; to this day I've never seen anyone quite so enthusiastically possessed by his identity as a writer.

When he died four years later, just before the publication of his 1,485-page, two-volume *Complete Poems,* it seemed inevitable that—after a long career filled with detours, unexplained lacunae, political tempests, and not infrequent public bickering—he would be more widely acknowledged as one of the great poets of the century. Since then the usual academic undergrowth of critical studies and bibliographies has proliferated, but the work itself has found only a peripheral audience. Readers have been deterred by the daunting scale of his poetry and its multitude of surface difficulties, but more fundamentally by its unobtainability; mostly we've had to make do with cutouts, imports, or inadequate selections. Penguin's paperback edition will for the first time make the *Complete Poems* generally available; but it may not prove easy for the unprepared to find their way within this frequently disorienting compendium.

Most people who are aware of MacDiarmid at all know him by reputation as a proponent of Scottish nationalism and the restoration of Braid Scots as a literary language; yawn-inducing topics for the majority of readers. A glance at a single heavily glossed page of the early work will be enough to discourage many from proceeding. Yet MacDiarmid had curtailed his use of undiluted Scots by the early thirties, and his later poetry in English is not only accessible (despite its fantastically eclectic vocabulary) but comprises a body of ecstatic writing that evokes a twentieth-century Thomas Traherne or Saint John of the Cross. In little-known poems like "Diamond Body" and "In the Slums of Glasgow," MacDiarmid—an uncompromising atheist and loyal Communist—expresses a mystical ardor that outblazes the politer pieties of religionists such as Eliot and Auden. True to his materialist views, MacDiarmid confronts spiritual experience without the aid of dogmatic trappings or supernatural explanation: "I have not gained a single definite belief that can be put / In a scientific formula or hardened into a religious creed. / A conversion is not, as mostly thought, a turning towards a belief, / It is rather a turning round, revolution indeed." These great poems, however, are not neatly signposted: they coexist with cantankerous political tracts, etymological exercises, interminable catalogs of objects and phrases. The reader forges through brambles and bindweeds to come unexpectedly upon dazzling light and limitless expanses of water. The best point of entry into the *Complete Poems* is probably "The Kind of Poetry I Want," a thirty-three-page unfurling of MacDiarmid's aesthetics that embodies the poetic values it propounds. One may then be ready for "In Memoriam James Joyce," an extraordinary poem compounded of multiple dialects, jargons, bibliographies, literary and scientific extracts, interwoven to create a supreme homage to "Language, / Accomplishing what it pleases, traversing all things, / By subtlety of nature; rising to colossal dimensions, / Or standing on the tops of the filaments of a flower, / Or rising to the solar sphere on a sunbeam, / And commanding the three worlds."

These contradictory textures reflect their maker. It is one of the paradoxes of MacDiarmid's career that poems with the exalted harmonies of "Island Funeral" or "In Talk with Donnchadh Bán Mac an t'Saoir" should proceed from a man outwardly combative, opinionated, and—on the evidence of his collected letters—consumed by a manic compulsion to keep busy. He lived under pressure and apparently liked it that way. In an early letter he muses that "if . . . I could get a sufficient breathing space, then I think I could take stock and write myself forever out of the tangle," the tangle being "my continuing mental 'spate.' " His biography, however, doesn't indicate a person much given to breathing spaces. Born Christopher Grieve, the son of a rural postman, he was teaching Sunday school at thirteen, claimed to have read "upwards of twelve thousand books" by fourteen, and at sixteen had initiated his complicated political career by joining the Fabians. After serving with the Royal Army Medical Corps in Salonika (where he contracted cerebral malaria and witnessed the devastation of the 1918 flu epidemic), he simultaneously worked as a full-time journalist, raised a family, published a multitude of books, magazines, and pamphlets, served as town councillor and justice of the peace, abetted the general strike of 1926, and (under his newly adopted pseudonym Hugh MacDiarmid) wrote in rapid succession three volumes of poetry that more or less invented modern Scottish literature: *Sangschaw, Penny Wheep,* and *A Drunk Man Looks at the Thistle.*

In 1928 he helped found the Nationalist Party of Scotland, from which he would be expelled in 1933 for his Communist tendencies; he thereupon joined the Communist Party, and was duly expelled in 1938 for nationalist tendencies. (In 1956, in a move that was widely condemned, he rejoined the CP to express his solidarity with "the suppression of the threatened counter-revolution in Hungary.") Conscripted for national service in World War II, he worked as a copper fitter and later (after sustaining serious burns in an industrial accident) as a deck-hand on a Norwegian merchant ship. All that time he was living well below the poverty line, a situation alleviated only in 1950 by his receipt of a civil list pension for his services to Scottish literature. In his later years he maintained the same frantic pace: lecturing on William Blake in Peking, participating in the ban-the-bomb movement, standing for Parliament on the Communist ticket. He was certainly true to his early declaration of intent: "Other people can chew over niceties. I want to win through and do things—and will!"

The Letters of Hugh MacDiarmid, in its nine-hundred-odd pages, chiefly conveys an impression of breathlessness and bustle. These are not literary letters: no one reading them would deduce the qualities of the poetry. The whole huge volume contains barely any extended description or emotional revelation or even wit; he hasn't time for such things; he writes to take care of business, exhorting to political action, rounding up contributors for his countless editorial schemes, offering the occasional necessary condolence, begging (with humiliating frequency) for financial assistance. He's in too much of a rush to expand on his ideas, and simply refers the correspondents back to his other writings. He apologizes for his brusqueness, but, as he explains to one friend, "this is my 40th letter tonight and I am ink-sick." Mostly he talks about what he is writing, and the enumeration of works in progress leaves little question about why his letters are so perfunctory: in 1935 he notes, "I have no fewer than twenty new books—prose and poetry—on the cards and am devising my time-table to write them," and after finishing his autobiography in 1940 adds, "I'm tackling another at least as big—a huge survey and analysis of the whole field of Scottish personality throughout the ages. And besides that I have a vast amount of poetry on the stocks, a history of Scottish doctors and doctoring, a book on the Faroe Islands and a biography of John Maclean." Despite all manner of distractions, he published nearly a hundred titles in his lifetime.

Amid this turbulence, there's a glaring gap where we would expect to come upon personal feelings and intimate relationships. A few facts can be pieced together. His first wife left him for a coal merchant, and for several years he did not know the whereabouts of his children. He remarried, and in 1933 moved with his second wife and newborn son to a remote island in the Shetlands, where they remained for a decade and where much of his best work was written. There are hints of a drinking problem. In 1935—at the height of his productivity as a poet—he suffered a nervous breakdown: no details are given, but a photograph taken at the time reveals a face emaciated and terrifyingly remote. Within a year he was back in the fray, more pugnacious than ever, and there was to be no further parting of the veil draped over his private life. The letters make clear that he preferred it that way. Describing himself as an "Ishmaelite," he states baldly, "I do not like people—I'd be ashamed to profess any regard for the mass of mankind—I may love or have friendship for an individual here and there, but that is all. I am essentially a loner and practice what I preach. . . . I have always eschewed intimacy. . . . And I cannot see how it can be held that I have missed anything worth having."

MacDiarmid would have been enraged at an attempt to draw connections between the evident limitations of his emotional life and the rigidities of his politics, but it's hard otherwise to account for the strain of autocratic vindictiveness that permeates his ideological pronouncements. MacDiarmid's political tone recalls Ezra Pound's, even though one supported Stalin and the other Mussolini. (In fact, he shared with Pound—aside from mutual poetic admiration—a lifelong commitment to the Social Credit theories of Major C. H. Douglas.) One hesitates to place much confidence in someone who in 1929 called for "a species of Scottish Fascism," and who in 1950 remained convinced that "Communism . . . is the only guarantee of individuality in the modern world and the U.S.S.R. the only real democracy the world has yet seen." When MacDiarmid dons his Communist hat, his skeptical intelligence turns to jelly; like a Falwellite anticipating the Rapture, he talks of "the withering away of the state" as if it were an imminent event. In a revealingly naive letter he writes: "I am out for . . . an *International* United Front in Great Britain with the achievement of an autonomous Scottish Workers' Republic as one of its definite objectives. I am not unaware that I may have to fight this matter right through to the final court of appeal in Moscow itself. But I have been doing a course of very thorough and comprehensive political reading and feel fully equipped. . . . On whatever grounds I may be beaten at least it will not be able to be said that my line is not consonant with dialectical materialism." This was written in 1936, at the height of the Moscow trials, yet MacDiarmid appears to believe that he will prevail by brandishing his "comprehensive political reading," as if he were going up against a conference of logicians.

The personality that surfaces in the letters—obdurate, ideologically narrow, barely likable, with a penchant for defensive self-praise and venomous counterattack—contrasts strangely with the lucid, exultant, life-embracing character of the poetry. MacDiarmid himself was keenly aware that his poetry represented a triumph over personal identity—whereas in the letters we find, more drably, the identity triumphed over. Self-expression was never his goal: "I have no silly personal pride; I do not write poetry—I am merely the vehicle for something far greater than myself."

We can begin to read him properly by looking at his poetry not as a portrait of the artist but as a miniature cosmos, and the minutiae of politics, science, geography, and linguistics with which he crams his lines as mechanisms—like Homer's prophetic dreams and celestial messengers—for embodying ineffable substructures. Scientific materialism was for MacDiarmid what mythology was for the ancients and what Aquinas's theology was for Dante; and we don't need to accept the truth of his data any more than we need to believe in Zeus or Purgatory. If we take his huge poetic corpus as a single omnivorous epic, coherent although unfinishable, even the oddest details start to make sense: like his identification of Soviet Georgia as the prehistoric birthplace of Gaelic culture, and the resonance he extracts from its being Stalin's birthplace as well.

He wants to tie all odds and ends together, "like Fred Astaire, who has combined / All forms of dancing into one perfect whole," and calls for "A poetry in which the disorder and irrelevancies / Of the real world are seen / As evidence of the order, relevance, and authority / Of the law behind." MacDiarmid's poetic is geared to take *everything* into account, all the extraordinary hodgepodge of information accumulated in a lifetime of reading and observing:

> The limpets wandering about
> Grazing on fine encrusting weeds,
> And the acorn barnacles, the dog-whelks
> Grey-shelled

are in the poem not for their metaphoric significance but for the fact of their existence, their unfathomable multiplicity:

> Millions upon millions of them
> Hardly discernible here
> In the brilliant light in which sea and sky
> Can hardly be distinguished from each other.

His modest goal is to become the poet laureate of matter itself.

He began by becoming Scotland. Single-handedly he set out to give his homeland three things it lacked: a language, a modern literature, and a political identity. Language was uppermost, Scots—not Gaelic, but the Scottish variety of spoken English—had sunk to the level of a despised dialect, incapable of expressing much beyond provincial truisms, deprived of a vocabulary for scientific and intellectual concepts. Its last great literary exemplar was Robert Burns, who had been turned into a sentimental symbol of lost rural virtues. MacDiarmid looked back beyond Burns to the age of the makars, those fifteenth-century poets—William Dunbar, Robert Henryson, Gavin Douglas—whose Scots was a language as supple as Chaucer's or Ronsard's, reflecting an independent cosmopolitan culture more closely tied to France than to England. His self-imposed task was to invent a language in which poetry as great as theirs could be written, a synthetic Scots drawing on all eras and regions, and incorporating neologisms and foreign words where necessary. He first tried out the textures of his language in brief, delicately modulated lyrics:

> I' the how-dumb-deid o' the caul hairst nicht
> The warl' like an eemis stane
> Wags i' the lift.

Translated into Standard English, this becomes, "In the dead silent depth of the cold harvest night, the world like an unsteady stone wavers in the sky." In anthologies MacDiarmid is still represented mostly by these early poems.

From there he went on to a far more ambitious project, the book-length poem *A Drunk Man Looks at the Thistle* (1926), a tour de force that, owing to its difficulties, is more celebrated than read. It's the kind of work every young poet dreams of writing, a fluid, unsystematic poem undertaking "to deal with a diversity of ideas shooting from all directions on an intoxicated mind and be concerned only . . . that poetry is made of them." Pushing Scots as far as it can go, MacDiarmid excavates long-buried sounds and sets them dancing:

> The elbuck fankles in the coorse o' time,
> The sheckle's no' sae souple, and the thrapple
> Grows deef and dour: nae langer up and doun
> Gleg as a squirrel speils the Adam's apple.

A Drunk Man's eighty pages quiver with philological merriment, as the poet concocts a stew in which Robert Burns, Christ, Alexander Blok, and the history of Scotland slop up against the homelier ingredients of a night at the pub and a long walk home in the dark.

MacDiarmid was by now a national figure, leader of what had already been proclaimed the Scottish Renaissance, and his supporters would have been happy to see him continue indefinitely in the vein of his first books. He disappointed them by veering away from Scots—although he never gave it up altogether—and concentrating increasingly on English: not an English recognizably "poetic" but what Kenneth Cox describes as "the nameless nondescript English of journalists, universities and international communication: a cerebral lingo . . . understood everywhere and able to accommodate the artificial vocabularies of science." After immersing himself in the primordial linguistic ooze of home—"Or in the pyrnit fields that to ozmilt dwine / Or in the waters that rin, / Sae lang submerged but on the skyline / Kyth wips o' orphine afore they're din"—he moves toward a colorless, delocalized language, a language that enables the reader to focus on the "poetry of facts":

> A poetry like an operating theatre,
> Sparkling with a swift, deft energy,
> Energy quiet and contained and fearfully alert,
> In which the poet exists only as a nurse during an operation,
> Who only exists to have a sponge ready when called for,
> Wads of sterilized cotton wool—nothing else
> Having the smallest meaning for her.

The resultant "style without a style" is unlike anything else in English poetry; MacDiarmid was consciously writing in English as a foreign language, no longer even a Scot but a world citizen, a member in anticipation of the future civilization he saw himself building: "the impending task of mankind / Is to help to bring to a close the 'conflict' stage / Of the present process of the discontinuous / And to usher in the 'harmony' stage." Possessed of an absolute faith in his poetic vocation, he assumes that whatever he writes serves an ultimate purpose of which he remains necessarily ignorant. Consequently, he has no interest in "fine" or "controlled" writing: "My job, as I see it, has never been to lay a tit's egg, but to erupt like a volcano, emitting not only flame, but a lot of rubbish." The poem is not a diverting artifact but a zone of truth-telling, of prophetic statement. In this, like his two great contemporaries—the Welshman David Jones and the Northumbrian Basil Bunting—he embodies an attitude alien to the London-Oxbridge tradition of ironic detachment. What could be more astonishing—or, to some, more offensive—than a poet who says precisely what he means? MacDiarmid means to make himself understood: unafraid of banality, he will speak in the simplest language, he will repeat, elaborate, pile up analogies, make expressive gestures with meter and texture, he will above all go on as long as necessary to reach the reader's mind. He will if possible go on forever.

His long poems are sections of longer poems, themselves but segments of the one endless work variously called *Clann Albann, Mature Art, A Vision of World Language, Impavidi Progrediamur,* or *Haud Forrit.* The scale of his project seems at first glance elephantine—but an elephant, as MacDiarmid would be the first to remind us, is as delicate a creature as any other. Some writers impress by their purely literary merits: grace, concision, invention. MacDiarmid's work strikes first of all by its human qualities—straightforwardness, energy, sheer endurance—which in his hands become formal qualities as well. We respond to the obstinate seriousness of a voice speaking not to itself or to the dead or to an imaginary public, but to the individual sentient reader:

> Come, follow me into the realm of music. Here is the gate
> Which separates the earthly from the eternal.
> It is not like stepping into a strange country
> As we once did. We soon learn to know everything there
> And nothing surprises us any more. Here
> Our wonderment will have no end, and yet
> From the very beginning we feel at home.

The "Come, follow me" is not a rhetorical but a literal instruction.

This poetry hates closure, wants only to unfold, to branch out, to feel the air on it. Nothing is less quotable: it is vast not just in overall concept, but at every point. You must plunge in and swim for great distances to get the feel of it. Once he got beyond his early lyrics, MacDiarmid was no longer interested in just the sliver of moonlight on the ocean, but in the tidal pull, the contours of the shoreline, the position and philosophical prejudices of the observer, the chemical components of the brine, and the profusion of sea life below the water's surface. In order to create more time, more room for being, he dilates syntax, finds spacious unforeseen cavities within clauses, slows down the rhythm of the poem until each syllable seems enormous: "Impatience is a poor qualification for immortality."

He would not have been surprised that his inviting, wide-open structures have had so few visitors:

> . . . The widest open door is the least liable to intrusion.
> Ubiquitous as the sunlight, unfrequented as the sun,
> The inward gates of a bird are always open.
> It does not know how to shut them.
> That is the secret of its song,
> But whether any man's are ajar is doubtful.

MacDiarmid trusted he would find his readers in the egalitarian world society he saw emerging in the next century. However skeptical we may be about the prospect of such an earthly paradise, we can at least take pleasure in the verbal paradise he has left us as a token of it.

Is That All There Is?

The Morrow Anthology of Younger American Poets

A poetry anthology is a map, and hence exerts a disproportionate influence: what country you end up in depends on the scope and clarity of the available charts. The best such books—Donald Allen's *The New American Poetry,* for instance, or Kelly-Leary's *A Controversy of Poets,* or Quasha and Rothenberg's *America a Prophecy*—have been useful not so much for their standards of "excellence" (the current neocon catchword) but for the richness and strangeness of the territories they opened. Each proposed a multitude of directions, relations, unanticipated seams and cross-currents, and in so doing created possibilities for new work. A bad anthology, on the other hand, limits itself to the parameters of a well-traveled lake, chugging predictably from inlet to inlet, until we arrive where we embarked. *The Morrow Anthology of Younger American Poets* offers a textbook case in point, appropriately for a book that seems intended to be a textbook: a massive compilation of 531 poems by 104 poets that hauls us all over the fifty states without ever straying from the norms of academically respectable verse. The book is worth lingering over only because many readers, taking the title literally, will accept this as an adequate representation of what young American poets are doing. Quite the contrary: the editors' perspectives are so narrow as to exclude all but one wavelength of poetic practice. To confuse that wavelength with the spectrum is to confuse the Westport ferry with passage to Cathay.

Review of *The Morrow Anthology of Younger American Poets* edited by Dave Smith and David Bottoms (New York: William Morrow, 1985). Reprinted from *VLS,* June 1985.

While editors Dave Smith and David Bottoms insist that they don't regard this as "the presentation of an aesthetic statement," the book's overwhelming unity of tone speaks for itself. That unity is quite an editorial accomplishment, given the ample individuality displayed by some of these poets in other contexts. Here, however, you start to feel that you're reading the work of a single author, that composite younger poet whom the editors define in their preface: "He has one or more graduate degrees in literature or writing and teaches both in college. . . . He has been awarded a grant from the National Endowment for the Arts or the Guggenheim Foundation. . . . He is rarely a card-carrying group member, political or aesthetic. . . . He speaks Williams as fluently as he speaks Eliot, Neruda and Milosz as quickly as James Wright or Elizabeth Bishop. He seems to jog more than to write literary criticism."

The emphasis on academic credentials is extended by Anthony Hecht's blissfully complacent introduction ("Not so long ago it was held ruinous to the poetic sensibility . . . for a poet to hold a teaching position. . . . That curious attitude has long since disappeared") and by the list of diplomas affixed like a curriculum vitae to each contributor's photograph. The message is clear: *We* are now running the show, and no bohemians, political troublemakers, linguistic experimenters, or unschooled improvisers need apply. Hecht's backhanded slap at Ezra Pound and Robert Duncan for their "archaic diction" completes the picture of a homogenized, undisturbing eclecticism.

The Morrow Anthology amounts to a portrait of a milieu encompassing the mainstream university and commercial presses, and the prestigious writing workshops that feed them: that little universe which holds all the worldly glory an American poet can aspire to. It's a milieu that regularly certifies its own good taste by the distribution of trophies and honors: and in the absence of other criteria these honors play a major role in determining hierarchical relationships. As the anthology's jacket copy put it: "These younger poets have won an impressive array of awards, including Lamont prizes, Devins awards, Walt Whitman awards, Yale Younger Poet awards—more than thirty such awards, in fact." We are dealing, then with a display of officially sanctioned art, a veritable *poésie de salon*. The ambitious younger poet will find the book useful as a set of guidelines for writing a prize-winning poem. Before he rises to the bait, however, he ought to spend some sobering hours at the local library perusing books with titles like *Prize Poems of 1927:* they do not, as a rule, wear well.

The editors offer only a few clues to their method of selection, but they are revealing; the work chosen had to "exert an immediate, dramatic presence, possess a character of language that sustained and renewed our attention and demonstrated a treatment of subject that moved us beyond the subject to an enlarged and resonant awareness of being alive." The key phrases are "dramatic presence" and "treatment of subject." They point the way to the anthology's dominant mode: a naturalistic monologue in which an "I" —usually the poet, occasionally a carefully chosen persona—relates a personal anecdote, most often stemming from childhood or early youth. Whether the poet speaks (as in Larry Levis's "Sensationalism") directly to the reader ("I do not wish to interfere, Reader, with your solitude— / So different from my own") or, in a transparently rhetorical manner, addresses a lover or a relative or stranger on the street, the poem is wedded to the formal strategies of conversational speech. In a conversation there are numerous unspoken rules, things you may and may not do: you must talk *about* something, even if only the weather; you may not arbitrarily leap from perception to perception; you may not suddenly become someone else, or become no one at all; you may not abolish time or syntactical logic. But poetry thrives on sudden transformations and disjunctions, and is often happiest when it has least to talk about—as in those crystalline lyrics of Campion or Jonson that seem to delineate emptiness. The "I talk, you listen" format of the anthology poems eliminates at the outset whole worlds of potential discourse.

Although the primary stylistic layer tends in most cases toward photorealism, the bare object rarely stands alone. A second layer of more explicitly "poetic" language is superimposed on the first, in the form of unwieldy similes, stridently expressive verbs, and other standard-issue tools of the contemporary poet. There is rarely any danger in confusing the "subject"—the unadorned anecdote—and the "treatment" that has been pasted onto it. When Diane Ackerman refers to the "the eight-legged serialists / of the tented dawn" we know that what's meant is "spiders": the more fanciful phrase does not seriously propose an alternate reality. Thus we get poems that resemble convoluted paraphrases, where "form" and "content" can be neatly pried apart like one of the clamshells that figure so heavily in these poets' imagery. (For some reason—evidently a personal predilection of the editors—the anthology contains at least twenty-three poems about fish, fishermen, or fish markets.)

The divide between matter and manner shows up particularly in the overuse of similes. Indeed, after wading through this book I'm ready to propose that the simile be abandoned altogether as a literary device, or perhaps relegated to private eye novelists. The endless marshaling of elaborate comparisons creates lines top-heavy with their own cleverness: girl scouts "spill out of the room like marbles" (Sharon Bryan), a water strider is "suspended / like a conductor's baton" (Brad Leithauser), and we come upon "orange lips / of fungus making the rotten log a portraitist's / day's doodling" (Albert Goldbarth). Figures of speech are also subject to the law of diminishing returns. I've never known what one is supposed to do with such tropes, except file them away in some ultimate lexicon of similes, where Rodney Jones's mosquito "kneeling like an old woman / With the proboscis of her prayer buried in the idea of God" might lie down with William Logan's seagulls "like winged burghers stacked up outside heaven," and the whores who "curve slightly, like plastic spoons / being worked in a hardening cheese dip" (Albert Goldbarth) might take sustenance in Daniel Halpern's "*trattoria* sprinkled like parmigiano over the city."

More fundamentally, these embellishments bury the natural object they are ostensibly trying to heighten. It's as if the elemental constituents of the world—waves, light, rain, wind, darkness—were insufficient in themselves and had to be dressed up in words in order to figure in a poem: so we get "insistent tragic waves" (Jorie Graham), "the massive argument of light" (Louise Glück), "a slow alphabet of rain" (Denis Johnson), "the obvious wind" (Sydney Lea), "the stupefying cup of darkness" (Edward Hirsch). Likewise when Reginald Gibbons writes of the "the great whelks / dashed and battered till hope / was the hollowness in their cold clean skulls" there is no question of the physical presence of the whelks—their *being*—actually entering the poem. They have simply been mobilized for rhetorical service, like the birds that kick off the same poem: "Give the mourning doves any sun / at all and they will begin to grieve." *The Morrow Anthology* defines an anthropomorphic poetry in which the nonhuman exists to provide metaphors for human feelings. No matter how outdoorsy the subject, the verbiage tends to get in the way of the vegetation.

A muted sense of spiritual crisis suffuses the book, and provides its chief interest. As the editors point out, their archetypal younger poet "is haunted by time and death yet God seems a minor problem." In practice this means a secular poetry for which myth functions only as literary echo, an ironic counterpoint to the emotional claustrophobia of daily life. In Michael Blumenthal's "Today I am Envying the Glorious Mexicans," for example, a gnawing self-consciousness longingly contemplates the abandonment it's debarred from: "I just want to emulate / the beautiful purposelessness of the flowers / and Mexicans! I want to be the perfect madman / without remorse or metaphor, without reflection." So in lieu of ecstatic release, we linger in this instance on a sentimentalized image of the exotic Other. This is but one of the methods proposed for dealing with a recalcitrant self that refuses either to open up or go away.

The loss of mythic dimension leads to an emphasis on the real-life identity of the poet. Presumably the stylistic mannerisms are meant to be redeemed from preciosity by the "dramatic presence" of the author: the inescapably personal nature of what is being related, the persistent assertion that these are real wounds being displayed. The underlying statement often sounds like: "I suffered, but I made a beautiful poem out of it," couched in such viscerally autobiographical terms that the reader feels guilty about rejecting the poem. In its most extreme form this mode verges on emotional blackmail, as Susan Ludvigson comes close to acknowledging: "It's like poems you hope / will be read by someone who knows / they're for him and cry / at what he did or didn't do, / wishing to touch your face once more, / to cradle your body." In this diminished version of the confessional vein we find not the extravagant vices and manias of the Plaths and Lowells, but a more ordinary blend of glum self-pity and rueful nostalgia.

Reminiscence dominates in a way that is rarely fruitful, tending as it does to deflect attention from the verbal immediacies of the poem: "It is so quiet. It is 1957" (Greg Pape). "My parents couldn't know, in 1950, / how little they cared for coaxing roses / and patchy lawns from baked clay" (Sharon Bryan). "When I drink it is always 1953" (Lynn Emanuel). "They look a little like the trees I sat beneath in 1959" (Leon Strokesbury). It's as if everything that really mattered happened back in a dim zone that the poet attempts to evoke with phases like "I remember" and "I recall." The words summon up snapshots, family outings, familiar local landmarks, achingly intimate memorabilia, and elevate them into icons of a private emotion the poem intends to embody. Powerful feelings are acted out to prove the poet's sincerity, as if poetry were a form of therapy: yet the reader, for whom only the words exist, is conscious of nothing but a diffuse and ill-defined gesture. The present moment is tied down by past associations, just as language's potential freedom is hobbled by the demands of personal identity. Once again this leads to a limiting—in advance—of the poem's field of action.

There are, naturally, exceptions. Were I doing a poet-by-poet rundown, I might single out a dozen or more engaged in something quite different from what I've been describing. What concerns me is the book's residue, its overall tone. Nor am I implying that there's no room for the kind of poetry Smith and Bottoms have so relentlessly focused on: simply that there are a myriad of other poetries, the secret of whose existence they guard as closely as the Manhattan Project. If their anthology is ultimately indigestible, it's because of the ingredients they've left out.

Considering all the things a poems might be—song, epigram, hymn, koan, healing chant, political exhortation, ballad, newscast, snapshot, mantra, acoustical experiment, imaginary landscape, explosion of sheer spontaneous nonsense—the book settles for an amazingly standardized definition. The poems even *look* the same: they are neither too short nor too long, calling to mind the length preferred by academic poetry magazines and by poetry contests that specify not less than twelve or more than forty lines. The implications of this transcend the technical; both very brief poems and inordinately extended ones necessitate stances—ranging from egolessness to multiple personality—excluded by the premises of this anthology. The formal conventions espoused by Smith and Bottoms reinforce and are reinforced by a particular model of human psychology.

Beyond all else, the crucial missing element is music. True, the poems have a rhythmic structure, but it's the rhythm of essay or oratory rather than song. We find plenty of pregnant pauses, wry caesuras, and self-admiring punch lines, but precious little of what Ezra Pound called "a shape cut in time." The formal dance of poetry—its architecture of cadences and vowel harmonies, its syncopated weft-work—is too often reduced to a chopped prose, sometimes, as in these lines of Dave Smith's, more awkward and meandering than a competent novelist would permit himself: "How many hours must / a man watch snow shift the world before he sees it is only a dream / of useless hope stamped and restamped by the ash-steps of those we / can do no justice to except in loving them?" This aural monotony is the anthology's least forgivable aspect, ignoring as it does the scores of contemporary poets working richly in the area where language and music interact, where syntax oscillates between meaning and pattern: poets as radically different from one another as Michael Palmer, Rachel Blau duPlessis, August Kleinzahler, and Susan Howe give the lie to Anthony Hecht's statement that the anthology's poets "are of a generation that seems disinclined to sing," a characterization that only certifies Hecht's disinclination to listen.

The truth is that if you really want to know what the younger American poets are up to, you won't find it in a conveniently packaged take-home form. Legwork is required: you must scour the magazines, rummage through the chapbooks, haunt the bars and churches, keep your ears turned to the radios and record players. It may not be a golden age, but it's a feisty enough time, open-minded, critical of received forms, and diverse beyond *The Morrow Anthology*'s imaginings.

Ovid in the Video Parlor

August Kleinzahler

Some poets demonstrate their seriousness in obvious ways: they embark on multivolumed epics, or construct elaborate sequences according to mathematical schemata, or undertake to dismantle the architectonics of post-Platonic thought. Now that Theory reigns among us, such bravura displays of intellectual ambition have become increasingly common. Along comes August Kleinzahler, a fellow from Jersey City who writes on a deliberately small scale about smokestacks and Corn Doodles, haircuts and hollyhocks, love and wine, and does so in language that veers jauntily from video parlor argot to Ovidian tropes. *Storm Over Hackensack,* a compact collection of eighty handcrafted, sinuous, intensely focused poems, indicates both that subject matter still has its uses and that recent death announcements for the personal lyric were slightly premature. Not many writers, however, will have either the wit or the fluent technical inventiveness to follow in Kleinzahler's track.

The vocabulary strikes us first. We come upon words and objects, quite ordinary in themselves, that seem not to have been used before. Kleinzahler picks up contemporary debris as avidly as ancient artifacts: "Ten mighty condos suck / amperes / under pink night sky" in one of his distinctive cityscapes; by the end of the poem, moving back in time, he restores a place where "a branch crackling / set off a hubbub of frightened starlings." The poem's point is simple enough—a quiet spot on the river has been rezoned into gaudy monumentality—but the effects

---

Review of *Storm Over Hackensack* by August Kleinzahler (Mt. Kisco, NY: Moyer Bell, 1985). Reprinted from *Village Voice,* August 20, 1985.

extracted from "amperes" and "hubbub" elude paraphrase. Elsewhere, the casual juxtaposition of "sweatsocks," "Nepenthe," "sawbuck," and "skalds" establishes an idiosyncratic verbal geography. For Kleinzahler there is something hilariously strange about words like "noggin" or "cummerbund."

The words don't merely float in a textual Neverland: they pertain to actual places like "Sal's Paradise Club" and "Safeway's parking lot" and the Gimbel's luncheonette where a spectral Edward Hopper contemplates "the pink swivel chair / and the doughnuts under glass." Certain settings obsess Kleinzahler, and he doesn't so much describe them as haul them bodily into the poem. The TV repair shop with its "gallery of Zeniths in half-light" and the worn street filled with "air-borne grains of pizza crust" receive a magical life from the decorative arabesques lavished on them. On closer inspection the veneer of representationalism looks more like the ritualistic stylization of a praise-song in which names determine essences. The world is made for the poems; Citicorp exists so that Kleinzahler can use the word "pentahedron."

The all-American postmodern flatness of the landscape he sketches comes as no surprise, but the music Kleinzahler makes from it has unexpected resonances:

> Red pulse the big jet's lights
> in descent.
>   The aerial
> on the plumber's duplex shakes.

The subject is Newark Airport, but from cadence and texture we might deduce a hymn to the glory of God. The structural beauty of the lines persists regardless of any ironic or parodistic reading. The poem goes about its arcane harmonic business while the figures in the poem—like the "gentleman / in Italian loafers" who "will bring / profound good news / to a steak joint in Moonachie"—carry on independently with their own mundane affairs, indifferent to the unaccountably mysterious connotations of a word like "Moonachie." An eloquent melody—as in "An Autumnal Sketch"—may couch an exuberant joke (here, the piteous ineffectuality of certain poetical professors); the transcription of a stretch of urban roadway, in the wonderful poem called "From FDR Drive the Children of Whitman Gaze Up," becomes almost unnoticeably a treatise on the nature of reality.

With its balletic tricks of balance and precisely modulated humors, *Storm Over Hackensack* belongs on the same shelf with Paul Blackburn's *The Cities* and Carl Rakosi's *Ex Cranium, Night:* books that play a double game, adhering to the world's appearances all the better to metamorphose them into the poem's perfect dream-life. Kleinzahler ranges in mood from the goofy to the mournful, but always what concerns him is the shape of what he makes, the way the small parts dovetail into a song that can "jiggle stuck syllables till the sow / drops piglets." Like an ethereal mechanic he devotes himself to the concentrated work of distilling "sweetness / so rare / so minor a key were it music / if fabric / would come apart in your hands."

Songs for the Journey

Lorine Niedecker and Basil Bunting

Poets are constantly exhorted to "find their own voice," but for all the thrashing about and self-searching, the language of most poems comes out flat, generic, interchangeable. In the academies and urban centers and pages of little magazines, the voices overlap and blend. Perhaps the poets listen too much to each other. A truly idiosyncratic voice—a voice with what used to be called *character*—would need some space around it, some silence in which to nurture its distinctive branchings and coilings. Consider Basil Bunting and Lorine Niedecker: holed up in small corners of the universe, far from the markets where reputations are traded, each spending a lifetime to make, line by line, a small durable book of poems. "Only the rejected by men," Bunting once said, "can keep either truth or beauty in view"—not a martyr's pose but a cool statement of fact.

Ignored by most critics and readers, each of them recognized the other's singularity. He saluted her as "the best living poetess"; she reciprocated with a "Ballad of Basil" in which he sets sail with Villon and Dante and "the Persian Firdusi" for companions. Once, en route from his home in Northumbria, he dropped in on her amid her Wisconsin isolation. His manner, she noted, was "timid and tender," and he asked forlornly if it would be possible to get a glass of beer in the tea room she led him to. One afternoon out of a lifetime. They had worked so quietly in the world that Niedecker's death in 1970 went unrecorded in the *New York Times,* where Bunting's passing elicited

---

Reprinted from *Village Voice,* January 21, 1986.

little more than the expected comment about his being acquainted with Ezra Pound.

They were linked by their connection with Louis Zukofsky—who included a somewhat reluctant Bunting among the original Objectivists, and whose 1931 issue of *Poetry* catalyzed Niedecker's sense of poetics—but unlike Zukofsky, neither had much taste for theoretical formulations. Bunting defined poetry as a "flow of noise," Niedecker as "depth of emotion condensed," and otherwise they left such matters to the more metaphysically inclined. Their writing was local, concrete, and absolutely individual: not the individuality of a confessionalist ego but the impersonal solitariness of a mind wholly given over to its perceptions. They did not simply take up a given language and use it to describe something. In their hands, language itself metamorphosed under the weight of elemental presences: flavors, textures, geological strata, abrupt patches of vegetation. Each of them evolved something like a private dialect of English, a linguistic mode not obscure but gnarled, weathered, worn smooth in unpredictable places.

They approached poetry as a practical job of work, its tools obdurate, its material elusive. Both Bunting and Niedecker on occasion compared a poem to a fishing net, an empty structure trapping what it can of light and air and natural noise. The craftsman's trick is to know just what waters to drop the net into, and when to haul it up: slow, precise work requiring silence, sharp reflexes, wide-awake senses. It's a poetry grounded in this world, not any transcendent other, and its methods and effects are unavoidably material. "The moment you leave off into abstract words," remarked Bunting, "you lose touch, with the reader and the music and the world. So stay away from Plato." Niedecker described her conception of poetry in physical terms: "I'd say mostly, of course, cadence, measure make song. And a kind of shine (or somber tone) that is of the same intensity throughout the poem. And the thing moves."

Lorine Niedecker—a fisherman's daughter for whom net imagery was autobiography rather than metaphor—lived for most of her years in an island cabin on Lake Koshkonong, Wisconsin. Her work might be summarized with the title of one of her poems: "My Life by Water." It's all one "sublime / slime- / song," heavy with mud and frogs, periodically submerged by floodwaters:

I grew in green
slide and slant
        of shore and shade
                Child-time—wade
thru weeds

or, elsewhere:

I rose from marsh mud,
algae, equisetum, willows,
sweet green, noisy
birds and frogs

Her marshland is as distinct a poetic landscape as this century has given us, fertile and destructive, its boundaries fluid, its inhabitants prey to a permanent uncertainty in the face of "Springtime's wide / water- / yield." There are no possessions that can't be swept away without warning. The seepage even invades the perimeters of personality: "My life is hung up / in the flood / a wave-blurred / portrait." Momentary fragments of intense knotted interrelation—"mossed / massed quartz / on which spruce / grew dense"—emerge from the water's obliterating rush:

I met him
We were thick
We said good-bye
on The Passing Years
River

Paradoxically, this clear-eyed poet of nature was at the same time elaborately literary, filling her lines with quotation and allusive wordplay. The writings that most influenced her—she cited among others Zukofsky, Dickinson, Thoreau, Lucretius, haiku—were for her part of nature, an inward extension of landscape. A poem could be built with any materials; her later poems include complex collages constructed from the words of Thomas Jefferson, William Morris, and Charles Darwin. There as elsewhere, she displays a builder's joy in formal placement. Structural integrity becomes a model of happiness, and her patterned surfaces swarm with decorative beauties, with playful echoes of nursery rhymes and folk tunes, with uncanny approximations of the most diffuse and gossamer phenomena. The way the words fit together implies some kind of contentedness. Yet her poems have an emotional force like the breaking of an oppressive silence. Within their elegance, at its core, we become aware of a ragged, raging splendor, neither tranquil nor polite.

For most of her creative life she lived alone. Few of her neighbors even knew she wrote. For half a decade, while distant literati were comparing her to Sappho and Ono no Komachi, she supported herself by scrubbing floors at the local hospital. At sixty she married ("I married / in the world's black night / for warmth / if not repose"), traveled a bit on the Great Lakes and in the Black Hills, made herself available to the students and younger poets who were beginning to get in touch. But all in all it was an impeccably solitary life. A small circle of writers—Cid Corman, Jonathan Williams, Stuart Montgomery—praised her, published her, and gave her what sense she had of connection to the larger literary world. By choice, however, she kept herself apart from that world. Turning down a writer's dinner invitation, she wrote: "Fate usually intervenes to keep me from being socially active. . . . But fate has worked hand in hand too with my writing life—I don't mourn the lone-ness of it for poetry. In fact, I wouldn't do it any other way and I have the presumption to feel that others writing should retire unto themselves deeper than they do."

Much contemporary poetry takes the form of a discourse among intellectual peers. The mind on the receiving end is in some sense known, a friendly quantity. Niedecker's work differs in function; it's not so much a discourse as a meditation between herself and the speechlessness of what surrounds her. Ultimately she was her own audience, the poem not self-expression but a space she could inhabit, handmade like her cabin on Black Hawk Island. The problem in her poems is how to make oneself compatible with the sheer blind otherness of the natural world. No matter how graceful her ferns and water lilies, the waters are rooted in death. In the great extended sequences—"Lake Superior," "Traces of Living Things," "Paean to Place," "Wintergreen Ridge"—she kept returning to a point of mineral quiescence—

> In every part of every living thing
> is stuff that once was rock

—not in ecstasy but to attain a minimal point of equilibrium, where her mind could bring itself into tune with the mindlessness of matter:

> the wave-line
> on shell, sand, wall
> and forehead of the one
> who speaks

Lorine Niedecker distrusted poetry readings, preferring the subtler music of the inner ear to the theatricalizing encouraged by a live audience. ("How would the bug on the branch, walking to the end of it, or the raindrop there—your poems—be read to a hall filled with people?" she asked in a letter to Cid Corman.)

Basil Bunting, on the other hand, insisted that his poetry could be fully experienced only if sounded out loud. For him a poem's published text was little more than a musical score, lifeless unless performed: "A poem is a series of sounds in the air, just as music. Other things can be included or loaded onto it, but the essential thing is just the *noise.*" A recording exists of Bunting reading his masterpiece "Briggflatts," so we can hear its parallel assonances and craggily knocked-together consonants precisely as intended. But Bunting, regardless of his intentions, is just as much a poet for the eye. The mere sight of phrases like "rut thud the rim" and "pricked rag mat" and "fellside bleat," stacked up in a firm rough-hewn structure, creates a kind of orthographic landscape. In Bunting the words seem to have just been unearthed: here and there his vocabulary has been scratched by glaciers, dented by axes, buried under generations of rotted leaves. The words are no one's personal property.

The *Collected Poems* is at once remarkably slim and remarkably dense. It was Bunting who, in a German-Italian dictionary, came across the definition that Ezra Pound promptly adopted as a maxim: "*Dichten* equals *condensare*," i.e., to write poetry is to condense. Bunting compresses immensities of experience into clipped, tightly stitched lines. The miniature epic "Briggflatts" is only twenty-two pages long, but in the mind it expands to infinitely greater length, as if a lifetime's duration were somehow secreted within and between its syllables:

> Who sang, sea takes,
> brawn brine, bone grit.
> Keener the kittiwake.
> Fells forget him.
> Fathoms dull the dale,
> gulfweed voices . . .

When words are given their true weight of inherited connotation, they become heavy indeed: "Pens are too light. / Take a chisel to write." Although Bunting described "Briggflatts" as "an autobiography," the reader will find in it no chronicle of his evidently adventurous life. Bunting's reticence has kept us from learning much about his imprisonment for draft resistance during the First World War, his friendships with Pound, Yeats, and Ford Madox Ford, his work for British intelligence, his long residence in Iran as foreign correspondent, his retirement to the Northumbrian birthplace in whose sights and sounds "Briggflatts" is steeped. The poem's a memoir without a memoirist, in which the word *I* is used sparingly and with shifting signification. The poet makes himself an instrument of the world, constructs a summing-up of earthly elements, a catalog of smells and colors, the distillation of life into essential—and often microscopic—perceptions.

Bunting's method had been established as early as 1925 in "Villon"—

> precision clarifying vagueness;
> boundary to a wilderness
> of detail; chisel voice
> smoothing the flanks of noise;
> catalytic making whisper and whisper
> run together like two drops of quicksilver

—and honed in the abrasive satires of the early thirties. After nearly two decades of silence came "The Spoils" (1951), with its panoramic scope and soaring music, an homage to the classical Persian culture from which Bunting had drawn so many of his aesthetic imperatives:

> A fowler spreading his net
> over the barley, calls,
> calls on a rubber reed.
> Grain nods in reply.
> Poppies blue upon white
> wake to the sun's frown.
> Scut of gazelle dances and bounces
> out of the afternoon.

Whatever else a poem might be, it had to be an artisan's work. The focus was form, not revealed truth: "I don't give a damn whether I falsify experience or not. I'm out to make a good poem. I'm not there to provide raw material for psychologists. . . . I have never supposed a poem to be organic at all. I don't think the thing grows, it's built and put together by a craftsman." The poem is to be approached as a free-standing artifact, without regard to its essentially irrelevant maker. Bunting would have felt quite comfortable as one of the poets known to us as Anonymous.

He had little interest in intellectual originality, and suggested that "poets are wise to do as they usually do and stick to commonplaces." Insofar as the content of his poetry can be summarized, it has to do with the most ancient of perceptions: the body's frailty, the futility of desire, the ramshackle unsteadiness of human works. He was a great nature poet obsessed by the heartlessness of nature; his "gay thrush" sings of "familiar things, / fear, hunger, lust." "Chomei at Toyama," his wonderful poetic adaptation of the twelfth-century Japanese prose composition *Hojoki,* starts in a vein of Orientalist prettiness (no one was prettier than Bunting when he wanted to be), only to crash abruptly through the exotic spell:

> Empty markets, swarms of beggars. Jewels
> sold for a handful of rice. Dead stank

on the curb, lay so thick on
Riverside Drive a car couldn't pass.
The pest bred.

His reverence for the beauty of song did not disguise the sordid context of that beauty: quite the contrary.

The progress of Bunting's poetry resembles a homing in on his own roots. In the early work he writes as a voyager, a foreign resident. The settings are France, Germany, Japan, Iran. The music still echoes Pound and, beyond him, Dante and Catullus. Had he stopped writing after "The Spoils," we might remember him as a distinctive minor modernist. Instead—after another fourteen-year gap—he published "Briggflatts" at sixty-five, and thereby decisively changed the ear of the poets who came after him. It seemed nothing less than a resurrection of English poetry, with a fullness of body that had been so long lost as to become unimaginable:

. . . Unscarred ocean,
day's swerve, swell's poise, pursuit,
he blends, balances, drawing leagues under the keel
to raise cold cliffs where tides
knot fringes of weed.

The sensual delights of sound were themselves reborn, and through them, by implication, all the other senses:

Sycamore seed twirling,
O, writhe to its measure!
Dust swirling trims pleasure.
Thorns prance in a gale.
In air snow flickers,
twigs tap,
elms drip.

Swaggering, shimmering fall,
drench and towel us all!

It was a poem without high points, a continuously metamorphosing flow of sense impressions. Each of its elements, considered separately, shone keenly and icily clear, yet at the same time blended into the malleable current of the whole, in a triumphant vindication of Bunting's formal concerns. He never again published anything on that scale, but in a series of brief odes continued year after year to perpetuate the lingering harmonics of "Briggflatts." The last lines of one might serve him as epitaph:

> Stones indeed sift to sand, oak
> blends with saints' bones.
> Yet for a little longer here
> stone and oak shelter
>
> silence while we ask nothing
> but silence. Look how clouds dance
> under the wind's wing, and leaves
> delight in transience.

The words might be a belated commentary on what Lorine Niedecker had written ten years earlier: "Man / lives hard / on this stone perch / by sea / imagines / durable works." For both of them, poetry was an attempt to wrest something permanent out of the world's flux. They knew better than to crave eternal monuments against the certainty of dissolution. They could offer only a small song packed with essentials as if for a long journey.

Media Kids

The Poetry of the Brontës

The legend of the Brontës is one of the secret wellsprings of the modern conception of childhood. The gradual revelation of their hidden anomalous lives, initiated in Elizabeth Gaskell's *Life of Charlotte Brontë* and extended by generations of rummaging scholars, may have been one of those apparently low-key events that signal a radical imaginative shift. The buried complexities and passions of childish experience—the skein of loyalties and ceremonies and invented languages—emerged into daylight like the excavation of a forgotten gateway. *Jane Eyre* and *Wuthering Heights* had already imposed their uncomfortable presence despite all odds; springing without pedigree from the Yorkshire outback, they had forced their way into the grown-up house of literature. The sense of intrusion and enthrallment those books occasioned can be deduced from the subsequent canonization of their authors. Like many saints, the Brontë sisters embody demonic forces insistent on placation.

With their pallor and unworldliness—lost without each other, and needing no one else—they must have seemed a kind of mutation. "I used to think them spiritless," a neighbor commented, "they were so different to any children I had ever seen." The almost numinous awe they elicited is clear from Mrs. Gaskell's account: "The family with whom I have now to do shot their roots down deeper than I can penetrate. I cannot measure them, much less is it for me to judge them." Yet if they were at first characterized as abnormal—sequestered, precocious, "grave and

---

Review of *Selected Brontë Poems* edited by Edward Chitham and Tom Winnifrith (Oxford: Basil Blackwell, 1985). Reprinted from *VLS,* March 1986.

silent beyond their years"—the Brontë siblings would finally serve as models for a new kind of child, knowing, poker-faced, and conspiratorial, congenital outsider and secret magician. This kind of child, instead of growing up, becomes an artist. Making poems or paintings is an occult method for keeping alive an endangered private world while fending off the other, outer one.

The rudiments of their story—the parsonage ringed by gravestones at the edge of a vast moorland, where six motherless children (soon reduced by consumption to four) roamed in desolate freedom, turning their already Gothic surroundings into the scenery of a collective open-ended fantasy—set the tone for a whole subgenre of children's literature, in which fugitive innocents band together to reinvent the world on their own terms. When the world came, belatedly, to inspect the domestic life of the Brontës, it discovered the remnants of a perfectly formed miniature culture. Media kids in an age when the essential medium was literature, the Brontës took the materials shipped in from the remote great world—Shakespeare, Byron, Scott, sermons, ballads, hymns, the Tory political speeches their clergyman father recited at table—and transmuted them into a sort of luminous nest closed to outsiders.

That shared playtime universe was a zone of pure potentiality, where the children could create and exchange and eradicate personas: warriors and lovers, traitors and penitents, seers and ghosts and vengeful monarchs. At thirteen, in solemn tones worthy of an ancient Japanese chronicle, Charlotte described the evolution of their underground theater: "Our plays were established; 'Young Men,' June 1826; 'Our Fellows,' July 1827; 'Islanders,' December 1827. These are our three great plays, that are not kept secret. Emily's and my best plays were established the 1st of December, 1827; the others March 1828. Best plays mean secret plays; they are very nice ones. All our plays are very strange ones." From the plays in turn sprang novellas and poems, an endless floating history of the kingdoms of Angria and Gondal. Nor was this a passing fancy. Years later, working far from home as a teacher, Charlotte was still beguiling her leisure hours with long plunges into Angrian make-believe, to such an extent that the power of these waking dreams began to disturb her. In 1846 Emily and Anne (by then in their mid-twenties) continued, in a cheerier vein, to spin out the Gondal saga: "The Gondals still flourish bright as ever I am at present writing a work on the First Wars. . . . We intend sticking firm by the rascals as long as they delight us which I am glad to say they do at present."

Outside the nest, of course, the family did not fare well at all, quite apart from their horribly early deaths. (Charlotte, dying at thirty-nine, survived her younger siblings by more than half a decade.) Branwell, the great hope because the only boy, aspired to greatness in every sphere imaginable but achieved nothing more than a swift descent into alcoholism. Anne, shy and devout, was appalled by the spectacle of cruelty and blind appetite she perceived in what lay beyond Haworth parsonage. Charlotte, the only one to experience any worldly success, remained as isolated and anxiety-ridden after the triumph of *Jane Eyre* as she had been during her stints as governess and teacher. Emily balked altogether at being uprooted; her few brief forays into larger human society were followed by mute withdrawals to the homestead, where her favorite companions were animals. (Once she allowed a strange dog to bite her and then—furtively, to avoid alarming anyone—cauterized the wound with a hot iron.)

I linger on these details because no one is likely to approach the Brontës' poetry without some reference to the biographical subtext. The intensely personal nature of the poetry would demand such reference in any case. Charlotte mourns her sisters' deaths; Anne confronts her approaching end with a mixture of fear and submission ("A dreadful darkness closes in / On my bewildered mind"); Branwell memorializes the way stations of his downward spiral ("My body is oppressed with pain, / My mind is prostrate 'neath despair"); Emily, in a secret notebook, extends into adulthood the mapping of her island cosmos. This is above all a *private* literature, so much so that many of the poems—Emily's in particular—had to be divested of personal mythological trappings when first published. But no language can be truly private. A dream must be transcribed with the same vocabulary employed for shopping lists or handbooks of pedagogy. The world takes revenge on those who shun it, by making most attempts at private language appear pitifully derivative.

The Brontës did not wholly escape that fate, and even Edward Chitham and Tom Winnifrith, the editors of *Selected Brontë Poems*, seem loath to make excessive claims: "Because the Brontës wrote great novels their lives must be interesting, and because so much of their lives were occupied with poetry their poems must be interesting too." The logic of this bland demurral ought to be reversed: it's because of their preoccupation with poetry that their lives are interesting. Poetry was for them not a pastime but a definition of self. Everything about the way the poems functioned within the family is fascinating, not as tidbits of gossip for the Brontë Society, but as a close-up of what art is really about. That only one of the four, Emily, wrote great (and still extraordinarily underrated) poetry represents quite a good average, although it does mean that a volume such as *Selected Brontë Poems* has an inevitably disjointed texture. It's a long way from Emily's best to the weakest of Charlotte or Branwell.

In the language of poetry the Brontës sought imaginary freedom, imaginary power, imaginary companionship. Their cocoonlike structures nurture cherished insubstantialities. But a cocoon, to protect its vulnerable interior, must be to some degree impermeable. In the poems of Charlotte, Branwell, and Anne we see the evidence of desire and struggle, yet the poems, powerfully suggestive though they often are, seem for the most part shells rather than live entities. The available repertoire of Romantic symbols and effects proved insufficient to guard the transient essence. Each of them realized this and tried to find a way out of the impasse. For Emily no such problem existed. The way out was the way deeper into the interior domain she described in "To Imagination":

> So hopeless is the world without
> The world within I doubly prize,
> Thy world, where guile and hate and doubt
> And cold suspicion never rise—
> Where thou and I and Liberty
> Have undisputed sovereignty.

Her language and her dream-material were wedded, and their union resulted in some of the most obsessively beautiful poems in the language.

Charlotte, by contrast, may have achieved her literary identity precisely by freeing herself of poetry. Her true direction, culminating in *Villette,* was clearly toward the demystification of Romantic illusions. Dreams were in some sense the oppressor. "We wove a web in childhood, / A web of sunny air": this is apparently benign opening of one of Charlotte's most astonishing poems. But a web is at once a gossamer refuge and a menacing citadel, and those it protects are perhaps themselves imprisoned by it. As the poem proceeds, in its curious halting rhythm of advance and retreat, Charlotte discovers that the dreams of childhood, far from being dead, are alive within her and capable of taking her over completely. Fantasies within fantasies unfold with startling swiftness, until at last—where the poem breaks off rather than ends—Charlotte as such has ceased to exist, and we are astray on some Angrian battlefield where "Head-stones were reared in the waving fern."

Charlotte's best passages always envision tumultuous landscapes a bit too distant to be precisely described: "Deep in her isle-conceiving womb, / It seemed the ocean thundered, / And soon, by realms of rushing gloom, / Were seer and phantom sundered." Increasingly these landscapes are seen as something to be escaped from, as if her impulse to drench herself in internal imagery were at root a dangerous longing for annihilation. The once-alluring dream kingdoms grow jagged: "My dreams, the Gods of my religion, linger / In foreign lands, each sundered from his own, / And there has passed a cold destroying finger / O'er every image, and each sacred tone / Sounds low and at a distance, sometimes dying / Like an uncertain sob, or smothered sighing." As the sugar-candy palaces of versification broke down into near incoherence, the poet shifted away from a desire for 3-D fantasy toward the area where her real talent lay: the meticulous analysis of mental processes. To do so, it became necessary to dispel the false enchantment of daydream, and in effect to kill the magic of the poem. Maturity would be the prose of the fiction in which she dismantled melodramatic gestures and frillwork to find their bare core.

With Branwell we come to a more painful case, that of childish self-confidence attempting to bear up despite a growing awareness of failure. More than his sisters, Branwell in his early poems gives the impression of showing off. His blustery scenarios of storm and devastation provide not so much an imaginative refuge as a chance to display his poetic skill: " 'Tis He!—the Conquered Chieftain—he / Whose look could once give victory, / But sightless now— / The shot has torn his eyes away, / And his slashed face is gashed with clay / Cast backward in the eddying Flood / That washes off his bursting blood." It's not hard to picture him declaiming such lines in high histrionic style by the fireside. To the last he remained capable of hollow grandiloquence, as in the long, desperate ode on the death of Nelson, with its pitiable longing for the "endless fame" Branwell was to achieve, ironically, only by the accident of association. But in his last few years a bitter taste of reality began to infuse Branwell's rhetoric: "He whose hopes are o'er / Turns coldest from the sufferings of mankind. / A bleeding spirit oft delights in gore— / A tortured heart oft makes a Tyrant mind." A new objectivity, sharp but not quite strong enough to deflect him from his course, makes these final poems harrowing. He came so close to going much further.

Anne, on the other hand, appears from the start to have grasped both her gifts and her limitations. Alone of the four she exhibits no tendency toward Faustian overreaching, settling comfortably—and comfortingly—into a devotional mode more characteristic of the eighteenth or even seventeenth century. Technically a better versifier than Charlotte or Branwell, she tended toward an uncluttered simplicity of statement: "As in the days of infancy, / An opening primrose seemed to me / A source of strange delight." All her poems are in some sense religious. Even her most frustrated utterances take the form of prayer: "A heart whence warm affections flow, / Creator, thou hast given to me, / And am I only thus to know / How sweet the joys of love would be?" Like her novel *The Tenant of Wildfell Hall,* Anne's poetry often blunts its emotional strength with an overlay of predictable piety; she persuades herself but not necessarily the reader. Still, the faith she maintains at the last, in the face of imminent death, has an undeniable tenacity: "I've begged to serve Thee heart and soul, / To sacrifice to Thee / No niggard portion, but the whole / Of my identity."

These three poets have in common a piercing nostalgia for

the childhood dreams they shared, coupled with a growing awareness of the insufficiency of these dreams. For Charlotte the path lies from absorption in fantasy to self-analysis; for Anne, from egotism to worshipful submission; for Branwell, almost unwillingly, from grandiosity to bare disillusioned perception. Poetry, conceived as a fluid medium for preserving and broadening the spirit of childhood play, has in the end betrayed them. They would finally mistrust it as an opiate, an instiller of false hopes. In other words, none of them was fully a poet. They saw poetry as something previous to, or outside of, real life. Only for Emily were poetry and life indissolubly identified with each other. Where the others used words to tell stories or convey moral arguments, in Emily's poems the words achieve an imperious autonomy, breaking free of whatever narrative or logical framework might try to control them. Working at times close to the edge of nonsense, she captures the incantatory power of a nursery rhyme or lullaby:

> Waves above thy cradle break,
> Foamy tears are on thy cheek,
> Yet the Ocean's self grows mild
> When it bears my slumbering child.

Much of her poetry refers to a Gondalian context now largely lost except for cryptic subheadings like "R. Alcona to J. Brenzaida." While scholars have attempted to piece together the mythology, notably Fannie Ratchford in her reconstructed "novel in verse" *Gondal's Queen,* such efforts tend toward a pedantic literalism at odds with the spirit of the poems. The Gondal chronicles were evidently a freely invented, utterly unsystematic string of betrayals and assassinations and hauntings. We can hardly expect such an improvisational maze to yield hard-edged clarifications of what the poems are about.

In fact, the poems are mostly nonnarrative. They are not stories about Gondal, but literary artifacts written by Gondalians. Like the Portuguese poet Fernando Pessoa, who wrote under a variety of different names, each with its own personality, Emily Brontë obviously found it useful to speak in assumed voices. When the Brontë children were young, their father, wishing to gauge the mental abilities that he suspected they hid through shyness, had each of them wear a mask while he posed questions. Later, Emily's Gondalian disguises enabled her to utter what she might otherwise have chosen to hold back:

> I am the only being whose doom
> No tongue would ask, no eye would mourn;
> I've never caused a thought of gloom,
> A smile of joy, since I was born.

To speak through a mask is to reveal and conceal at the same time. The internal contradictions that result are the source of her poetry's strength. If Charlotte had to outgrow her childhood fantasies, for Emily it was necessary to grow *into* hers. The immersion in that mirror-world produced lyrics both ethereal and literal, withdrawn and spacious, obscure and simple. Her dream songs convey a paradoxical effect of earthiness and tangibility: "The giant trees are bending / Their bare boughs weighed with snow / And the storm is fast descending / And yet I cannot go." Emily exulted in that uncontrolled power of imagination which Charlotte sought to curb. In a poem written away from home, during her brief unhappy employment as a teacher of young children, Emily plunges into reverie not guiltily but with voluptuous enjoyment: "The mute bird sitting on the stone, / The dank moss dripping from the wall, / The garden-walk with weeds o'ergrown, / I love them—how I love them all!" The imagined scenes roll by, becoming more real than her physical surroundings, until the end of the rest period roughly calls her back: "I hear my dungeon bars recoil." The dream is the repository of all freshness, while ordinary reality is flat and false.

In daily life she was the most silent of the four; her poems teem with voices. She uncovers the voices *within* that silence, as if it were the center of a series of closed circles: the moors enclose the parsonage, the parsonage encloses the family, the family encloses Emily, Emily encloses silence. The silence, of course, encloses language, which in turn engenders all the rest of it as if for the first time. Thus Emily becomes the priestess of a self-invented religion. That air of secrecy and enclosure gives Emily the crucial role in the Brontë mythology. What the family as a whole was to the world at large, Emily was to the rest of the family: an isolation within an isolation. "My sister Emily," Charlotte wrote, in a passage that reveals how the mythologizing process began at home, "loved the moors. . . . She found in the bleak solitude many and dear delights; and not the least and best-loved was—Liberty. Liberty was the breath of Emily's nostrils; without it she perished." She hid her poems and, later, the symptoms of her illness, refusing doctors almost until the end.

The poems are a hermetic enterprise, reserving the right to be opaque and enigmatic. There is a voluntary blindness in them, an oracular groping that discovers unforeseen abysses and pockets of interior space. She writes to her own imagination, conceived as an active and alien presence within her: "Thee, ever present, phantom thing, / My Slave, my Comrade, and my King!" An ultimate privacy governs her poetry: "What my soul bore my soul alone / Within itself may tell." This sealed-in essence can of course be seen as pure negation, but for Emily it is a vital flame, "my intimate Delight— / My darling pain that wounds and sears / And wrings a blessing out from tears / By deadening me to earthly cares." She renounces the sun—"the hostile light / That does not warm, but burn"—to immerse herself in night: "Thought followed thought—star followed star / Through boundless regions on, / While one sweet influence, near and far, / Thrilled through and proved us one."

No writing could be more inwardly directed, yet in the heart of it we find not claustrophobia but expanses of air and rain. As the poet moves deeper into the coils of her imagination, the voices of wind and earth speak to her directly, urging her soul to return: "Thy mind is ever moving / In regions dark to thee; / Recall its useless roving— / Come back and dwell with me." The ritual overtones of these songs evoke a kind of home-baked shamanism, an effect heightened by the hypnotic ballad meter she tended to employ. An archaic form is best suited to trap the whisperings of ghosts.

Her poetry is all the more remarkable for the limited set of ingredients it's made from. Like the other Brontës, Emily drew on the elements of Romanticism that were ready to hand, and a hasty reading might easily confirm the minor status to which she has generally been consigned. Harold Bloom, for instance, in his study of Romantic poetry, does not even mention her. Her poems need to be read not merely for their passing felicities of melody—

> Fall, leaves, fall; die, flowers, away;
> Lengthen night and shorten day;
> Every leaf speaks bliss to me
> Fluttering from the autumn tree

—but for the profoundly original conceptions that propel them, hidden at times in the most deceptively simple forms. Hers is the poetry of a refusal to mediate between her vision and the world, a refusal to modify or compromise or translate into more accessible terms. What was within her outweighed the world:

> Then dawns the Invisible, the Unseen its truth reveals;
> My outward sense is gone, my inward essence feels;
> Its wings are almost free—its home, its harbour found;
> Measuring the gulf it stoops and dares the final bound.

Those lines are from a poem about a prisoner who forgets her cell by withdrawing into herself. In the next stanza the world forces its presence on her: "Oh, dreadful is the check—intense the agony— / When the ear begins to hear and the eye begins to see." There is something almost medieval in the tone, as if she were a Cathar mystic cast up in the wrong century. Elsewhere her visionary exactitude—as when she writes of "Time's withered branch dividing / From the fresh root of Eternity"—recalls the terminology of a Meister Eckhart. What at first seems blankness or vagueness in her writing often turns out to be a rigorously precise acknowledgment of the limits of language.

With almost inconceivable stubbornness she defends her right to imagine: not to escape but to cling fast to a hidden reality. Gondal is not an alternate world but the actual domain of her self. The liberty on which she insists is the liberty to remain as a child. She will not permit the world to sever her from her imaginative roots. Since in worldly terms this is an impossibility, she and the world must part company. Her life becomes an exercise in negativity, an absolute abstention. The only adequate language for such experience is the language of religious revelation, where meaning approaches as closely as it can to the border of silence:

> Though Earth and moon were gone
> And suns and universes ceased to be
> And thou wert left alone
> Every Existence would exist in thee.
>
> There is not room for Death
> Nor atom that his might could render void
> Since thou are Being and Breath
> And what thou art may never be destroyed.

The dissolving of all distinctions could hardly go further. In the unbroken flow of childish play, Emily had learned to accommodate anything, even the birth and death of the universe.

Shamans in Love
The Songs of the South

In the southern Chinese kingdom of Chu, which flourished about twenty-five hundred years ago, shamanism and political power were inextricably blended. It was a culture centered on religious forms that the northern Chinese already regarded as archaic—in particular, the spirit journeys on which the shamans embarked with the aid of ritual drumming and dance-steps. Their chants reconstructed a sacred geography linking the constellations of the night sky with a winding landscape of mountains, marshes, and rivers. To the deities nesting on clouds or in secluded inlets they directed amorous complaints—"The goddess comes not, she holds back shyly"—similar to the troubadors' ballads of disappointed love. These traditional incantations evolved into a species of court entertainment, and a later generation of poets took them as the basis for a sophisticated literary form. In the process, the already complex magical-erotic content of the songs acquired an additional layer of political allegory: the shaman jilted by the divine beloved became a virtuous statesman unjustly cast aside by his ruler.

Such is the conjectural history that David Hawkes extracts from the Chinese anthology *The Songs of the South (Chu ci),* compiled in the second century A.D. but written for the most part many centuries earlier. The essential figure in this poetic transformation was Qu Yuan, whose *Li sao* ("On Encountering Sorrow") is the anthology's cornerstone, and one of the primal

---

Review of *The Songs of the South: An Ancient Chinese Anthology of Poems by Qu Yuan and Other Poets* translated and edited by David Hawkes (Harmondsworth: Penguin Books, 1985). Reprinted from *Village Voice,* April 29, 1986.

events in Chinese literature. China already possessed a vast body of poetry, anonymously gathered in the earlier *Book of Songs,* but with Qu Yuan the individualized poet makes his appearance, transmuting inherited ritual into self-conscious literary artifact. Qu Yuan was himself the archetypal rejected statesman—Hawkes thinks he may have been a sort of shaman as well—and was said to have drowned himself after falling from favor with his monarch. The details of his career are lost in legend, but it hardly matters: *Li sao* is one of those fundamental articulations of consciousness—like *Prometheus Bound* or the Book of Job—in which we seem to encounter a living ancient mind, preserving itself beyond time in a structure of its own invention. We know Qu Yuan because he employed all his formalizing genius to make sure we would.

Li sao oscillates around an unstable binary center, the unresolvable disharmony between the poet and the Fair One who has spurned him. (The lack of clear gender identification in Chinese grammar allows the sex of the Fair One to remain ambiguous.) Like any rejected lover awash in rage and self-pity, Qu Yuan obsessively replays the circumstances of the breakup, recalls with cruel clarity his earlier hopes, while exonerating himself of any self-serving motivation:

> There once was a time when he spoke with me in frankness;
> But then he repented and was of another mind.
> I do not care, on my own count, about this divorcement,
> But it grieves me to find the Fair One so inconstant.

This ostensible humility is of course the reverse aspect of a furious pride: Qu Yuan knows very well that he has been rejected because of the sublime purity that sets him apart from all his fellows. His railings against his contemporaries resemble, in Hawkes's admirably full-bodied rendering, the invective of some biblical prophet:

> Truly this generation are cunning artificers,
> From square and compass turn their eyes and change the true
> measurement,
> Disregard the ruled line to follow their crooked fancies;

> To emulate in flattery is their only rule.
> But I am sick and sad at heart and stand irresolute:
> I alone am at a loss in this generation.

The poem culminates in a cryptic resolve to "go and join Peng Xian in the place where he abides," a line that may indicate either a withdrawal into occultism or a decision to commit suicide.

This emotional drama is enacted in an atmosphere thick with magical trappings. The multiple symbolism ranges from astronomy to music to herbal lore, while the structure follows the propulsive bounding movements of a shamanistic journey: "I watered my dragon steeds at the Pool of Heaven, / And tied their reins up to the Fu-sang tree. . . . / I looked all around over the earth's four quarters, / Circling the heavens till at last I alighted." While relatively compact, *Li sao* has an epic breadth. It might be read as an ultimate poetic response to the condition of powerlessness: subjected to the decree of an absolute ruler, the poet musters a whole cosmos of linguistic resources. Yet his triumphant display of mastery over music and language is at the same time an admission of failure and helplessness. The paradox of poetry—its simultaneous expression of fullness and emptiness—is already implicit in Qu Yuan.

The roots of his poetic can be found in the older "Nine Songs," which he may have edited, and in the extraordinary "Heavenly Questions," an ancient and fragmentary catechism whose very obscurity accounts for its fascination: "Toward evening there was thunder and lightning. Why was the lady sad? The high lord did not reveal his majesty. What was he seeking?" "What was the king's sorrow when he lay in hiding and lived in caves?" These riddles, to which the solutions have long since been lost, suggest the possibilities of an endlessly suggestive genre: the unanswerable question.

The later poems in the anthology are by and large imitations of Qu Yuan's mode; as the centuries pass, they become increasingly artificial and predictable. We have then, in one book, a complete cycle of literary history: origin, flowering, and decay. Hawkes charts the progression with wit and empathy; he is that infrequent blessing, a specialist with an eclectic mind who knows how to write. In his copious notes, side by side with dense technical discussions of textual problems, we find a fantastic wealth of historical and mythological data. Scores of potential books are secreted in the fine print of his commentary, and his prose encapsulations rise into flights of unexpected eloquence: "The soul of the drowned poet speeds from the watery gloom of the river-bed through crashing waves and rainbow-tinted mists to the source of the great river and thence to the summit of the World Mountain in an exultant burst of freedom in which the very boundaries of language itself seem to be broken." In *The Songs of the South* (originally published in 1959 but greatly expanded for this reissue) Hawkes has produced a translation both scholarly and passionate. It is basic reading for anyone who cares about where poetry comes from.

A Book of Music

Nathaniel Mackey

Why is modern American poetry different from other poetries of the English language? There are a hundred possible answers, but I suspect that jazz played the crucial role, at once goading and fructifying. The transformations it effected went well beyond the poetry-and-jazz experiments of the fifties and sixties. Even the music's richly suggestive iconography—from Jazz Age perceptions of a deliriously speeded-up mass culture to the postwar cult of bebopper as junkie visionary—accounts for only part of its influence. To gather all the poetry specifically "about" jazz (M. B. Tolson on Louis Armstrong, William Carlos Williams on Bunk Johnson, Amiri Baraka or Michael S. Harper on Coltrane, Sonia Sanchez on Pharoah Sanders, Paul Blackburn on Sonny Rollins, for a random handful) would be an impossibly encyclopedic undertaking, but the crux of the interchange goes past subject matter into the roots of sound and structure. The radical arc from Lester Young through Parker, Monk, and Powell to Coltrane and beyond was the most important factor in the working out of the new poetic measure. The poets gave the words a different weight because they had a different sound in their ears. As they tried to define what a free poetry might mean, jazz provided the most accessible model of a fully developed improvisational art.

Nathaniel Mackey's *Eroding Witness* reminds me of all this because, from its first syllables, it is drenched in music:

Review of *Eroding Witness* by Nathaniel Mackey (Urbana: University of Illinois Press, 1985). Reprinted from *VLS,* May 1986.

Waters
wet the
mouth. Salt
currents come
to where the
lips, thru
which the tongue
slips, part.

It's one thing to dedicate poems to Coltrane, Pharoah Sanders, or Don Cherry, to conjure up the Brazilian figurations of Elis Regina and Milton Nascimento or the splintered harmonics of Jimi Hendrix ("gigantic / seven-headed / snake, sticks out / one head at a / time. Must / be this hiss my / guitar's been / rehearsing"); Mackey pulls off the far harder task of doing with words what they do with tones. Unconsciously I found myself saying of one or another poem in the book, "I want to hear that again," as if it were a new album—and did in fact feel compelled to sound the lines out loud, to savor their slow spirals and quick piercing shortcuts:

The gummed hush of
watered grasses fondles our
unrest,   and as
outside the approach of
autumn scatters all
our unkept secrets
random winds unkink what
hints your hair
lets fall.

The fluid syntax enacts a stretching out, a physical flexing of language's fibers. The poems move through thickets of texture—"waters the colors of mud, thick / bush of hairs my bed / of stars" or "horsehairs / coiled in rain-/ water hiss" or "bambooish / odors of / bone"—toward sudden blinding flashes of "the wet sun" at the outskirts of the sayable. These self-invented rites (which evoke along the way the gods of Mali and Egypt and Babylon, the music of the Dogon, the power-stones of *santería,* the Xibalban underworld of the *Popol Vuh*) consciously seek to move *through* language to its far side. The quest leads not away from the body but into it. The poems remain rooted in the world, palpable and grainy, at once erotic and abstract.

A recent cosmological theory tells us that the universe is very likely a concatenation of oversized bubbles. This information reached me midway through *Eroding Witness* and proposed itself as a useful description of Mackey's approach to structure. The words seem the tensile outer skin of an otherwise imperceptible sphere, a skin adhering to the unseen shape that is the poem's real body: "Some say the waters washing Mali's / western edge are not the end of the world, / that the world is like a bottlegourd. / That a finger put at any point / on a bottlegourd / and pulled across its surface / comes at the end of its path to the / point where it started from." The implied interconnectedness means that anything can enter the poem, Anubis or acid rain, infusions of "luminous breezes" or "entrances of / unsought light," whatever is drawn into the field the poem uncovers.

"There I sit afloat in / the Boat of Years": The speaker is John Coltrane, at the Village Gate in 1965, about to launch into "Out of This World." The notion of song as journey, of poet as navigator, persists through the changes of *Eroding Witness,* but each arrival leads only to further movement forward, in a perpetually uncompleted churning: "Her splintered ships clog the sea of new / beginnings." You can move around inside this kind of music. Within the sounded notes you come upon ranges of latent echoes, "the frazzled edge of what remains 'unsung.' " Whatever other levels it operates on—mythical, sexual, political—*Eroding Witness* hinges on the precision and spaciousness of its acoustic geography.

Whole Edges

Clark Coolidge

There are accidents that happen to anyone who writes: odd wrong words, momentary dislocations, intrusions of uninvited and sometimes jarringly manic phrases. The words pull away from the meanings they've been roped to, until the writer feels tempted to abandon control and give them the freedom they seem to crave. Usually one resists that temptation. After all, there's a job of communicating to be done, an object to be described, a sentence to be driven toward its logical end. Yet restraining that impulse to babble can feel like a betrayal, a rejection of the source of language, the ground-tongue of which ordinary speech is a neatened, filtered, discreetly modified translation. Under normal circumstances we accept a language alienated from the world it purports to describe, a system running parallel to but never mingling, cut and dried and safely apart. But if we could climb down into language's inarticulate roots, we might stumble on the remote and ancient point where language and the world are joined. The prospect both terrifies and fascinates.

And if we did reach that point, what would we hear? Perhaps something like the speech that Clark Coolidge has been transcribing in book after book (eighteen volumes so far), patiently working against the grain of language-as-communication to find a deeper and cruder voice: "I walk down a street I see / I walk

---

Review of *Solution Passage: Poems 1978–1981* by Clark Coolidge (Los Angeles: Sun and Moon Press, 1986) and *The Crystal Text* by Clark Coolidge (Great Barrington, MA: Figures, 1986). Reprinted from *VLS,* June 1986.

into the bone." "Don't say the rock is a clot. It is a bend." "A shrieking in the woods of a leather bird / with wooden eyes." "Is it horrible to get inside a duck?" "I live by a wood-pulp chip-burner, like a vast / ash head or punk fleck, a thumb of incense / crystalled out large unavoidable as / mumps on a highway." "Dart that ate the tongue." "A poem is a sever." Coolidge's writing encroaches on the impossible language of dreams, a language that sweeps things together rather than discriminating among them, a language where any word can mean anything it wants to. We've heard it before; we hear it all the time, somewhere in the basement of our brains. But whoever notated it like this? "The bolds are entrance distills." "A tribute to strong green smear." Coolidge's work is neither surreal nor visionary; he practices an ultimate naturalism, an endless home movie of raw thought. We don't so much understand his words as recognize them, because they could be anyone's: "Things. . . . I still don't know / wholly what they are, any exact response. But I think / I always thought of myself as someone who improvises. / I didn't think of myself. I said to myself / I will make something up in a moment."

In his work it is always here and now. The same thing is always going on. Yet Coolidge mines an astonishing linguistic diversity out of the drone of mere presence. *Solution Passage,* which collects three years' worth of poems, runs to nearly four hundred pages—a stream of invention immediately followed by *The Crystal Text,* a single 150-page meditation on a piece of quartz. Either of these books by itself would be a peak; to be given both at once seems a natural wonder. Coolidge's capacity to work limitless variations on the theme of themelessness—"Thinking around things that edge me into / the blank thoughts"—makes him preeminently a writer's writer, someone who dares to take as his only subject the act of writing the next word, the blunt fact of utterance. His ancestors include Stein, Beckett, Williams, Kerouac, Jack Spicer, and the jazz musicians to whom he pays frequent tribute: "Streams of bop, antennas to no landing. / Stripes on a gasp of marveling. / The no note / end bone that collides standing lapses." What Coolidge does in language resembles Sonny Rollins constructing one of his interminable cadenzas, taking apart "Three Little Words" and putting it back together fifty different ways, always with the implication that there can be no end to the variations. Only the exhaustion of the improviser cuts off the flow of changes—and Coolidge, it appears, is tireless.

His art has another dimension, which the books can't convey: he reads his work aloud with a precision of pitch and a rhythmic control that are trance-inducing. In these live performances his words take on a different quality, as we cease to worry about what they mean and surrender to the mystery of their being there: "A life lived in primaries / a shout from the center of the light." Many poets nowadays are working with the mechanisms of language; the landscape is littered with disconnected signifiers and signifieds. Coolidge differs from most of his contemporaries by the intense and very untheoretical passion that animates his work, a passion that frequently manifests itself in wild humor ("A pile of hooted buckets. / A loose laugh spoon. / Miles of adroited pain paper") or in surges of a tactile lyricism: "I am in a hall, slope dome, full / catch of rains. A shying of the light / to a plaster fast if doweled slow. / And there is a note the lemon wouldn't. / Here is a clad doom." There's an implicit courage as well. In a way few writers would dare, Coolidge gambles on the blind faith that whatever happens in his mind is part of the world and hence of universal interest. Coolidge lays his thoughts on the line as if they were common property, a procedure that culminates not in solipsism but its wide-open reverse: "I am fascinated with the self / as it exists without one / active separation. / We are whole edges."

The Enjoyment of Being

Carl Rakosi

It has taken far too long—Carl Rakosi is eighty-three—but here at last are his *Collected Poems,* a monument so free from monumental posturings that its 490 pages could conceivably be read in a single delighted sitting. I can think of no contemporary poet who radiates such an aura of enjoyment—enjoyment of the senses, of the oddness of language, of the mind's capacity to make something out of nothing:

> If there is no connection between the wild
> hemp of Kashmir
> and the plectrum on a Persian lute,
> the mind
> will make one before the mallet comes down
> on the cymbalo.

So begins a poem characteristically entitled "Discoveries, Trade Names, Genitals and Ancient Instruments." Rakosi's unfettered range of association takes him readily from Finmarken to China to an eighth-century Ireland where "The ram leaped / and the seal disported on small rocks / and birds and geese cackled in the glen / and Castlekirk was built in one night by a cock and a hen." Lost imagined worlds surface continually from the humblest objects; an avocado pit is "darkened and faded / like an old Roman mural / from the bath house / of Menander." Words are permitted to lead a life of their own, so that at his merriest, in "The Glass of Madeira," Rakosi within a few lines

Review of *The Collected Poems of Carl Rakosi* (Orono, ME: National Poetry Foundation, 1986). Reprinted from *Village Voice,* January 13, 1987.

juxtaposes "Eskimo" and "placebo" and "limbic" before calling in Prospero, Beethoven, and his wife, Leah, for an exuberant windup.

At the same time the poet reminds us that "although he is fanciful, / he loves / salt and iron, / and absolutes make him belch." His poems thrive on a tensile oscillation between the particularity of raw data and the whimsical unpredictability of the mind's music. Rakosi can write with scientific precision of

> the jonquils whose air within
>   was irradiated topaz,
> silent as in an ear,
>   the stems leaning lightly
> against the glass,
>   trisecting its inner circle
> in the water,
>   crossed like reverent hands

—and then, following a twist of thought, let the metaphor carry him off into a sudden manic digression:

> (ah, the imagination!
>   Benedicite.
> Enter monks.
>   Oops, sorry!
> Trespassing
>   on Japanese space.
> Exit monks
>   and all their lore
> from grace.)

Although often inclined to make the poem an elegantly self-enclosed artifact, he lacks the hermetic solemnity to take the exercise altogether seriously. Abrupt shifts of tone and perspective become a technique for reminding himself where he is; the music of the spheres is prone to unscheduled interruption by honks, growls, and rude squeaks.

Rakosi's flair for comic deflation reflects his distaste for more grandiose strains of modern poetry. Commenting on Pound's *Cantos* he once remarked: "All that pretense and double-dealing are nauseating to me. And irrelevant. People today are not heroic, and modern human nature is not epic. It's just human, and anything else is just playing games." Rakosi's humor is multiform, ranging from the simplest burlesque and one-liners to elaborate parody and satiric dissection. Even the crudest jokes have their place, since Rakosi wants above all to be true to his own experience of himself. There is a time for contemplating island universes or Aristotle's poetics or the ravages of war, and there is a time for contemplating Calvin Coolidge:

His lips were sealed
tighter
than an old man's
scrotum
backing up from
winter water.

Rakosi strikes a balance of high and low, of pratfalls and philosophic flights, closer to certain medieval and Renaissance writers than to most current practitioners.

He has arranged this book not chronologically but by theme, assembling all the pieces into a complex self-portrait. In so doing he elides the curious structure of his career: his "Objectivist" writing of the twenties and thirties, culminating in the 1941 *Poems,* was followed by a twenty-year silence while he devoted himself to social work. His return to poetry in the early sixties generated an outpouring of writing more expansive and less calculatingly dazzling than in the earlier period. Between them, Rakosi and his friend George Oppen (movingly eulogized here in "The Old Poet's Tale"), whose career followed a similar course, testify to the rejuvenating effects of such prolonged sabbaticals. Rakosi's late phase is not so much a resumption as a rebirth. The "Ancient image" that he prays will "restore / my ancient relation / to words, / in which I have set / my hope" seems to have answered him generously.

These *Collected Poems* have a companion volume, a *Collected Prose,* issued by the same publisher a few years back, which admirers of the poems are advised to pounce on. It reveals the same virtues of humor, concision, and frankness, and established

Rakosi as a master of epigram: "When I sit down to write, I must not forget that one does not strike an attitude in front of a mountain." "The larger the crowd, the larger the rhetoric." "Not enough distinction is made between metaphors which transform a subject into poetry and those in which a poet escapes from his subject." Rakosi's daybooks are an indispensable adjunct to his work as a poet, a rich sample of the ground from which his clusters of particulars are culled.

A Modernist in the Mountains

Miyazawa Kenji

The Japanese poet Miyazawa Kenji, who died in 1933 at the age of thirty-seven, became a culture hero on the strength of a single brief poem written toward the end of his obscure and voluntarily impoverished life. "November 3rd"—an unpublished notebook entry probably intended more as a prayer than a poem—sketches a portrait of an idealized ascetic, "neither yielding to rain / nor yielding to wind," "without greed / never getting angry / always smiling quiet- / ly / eating one and a half pints of brown rice / and bean paste and a bit of / vegetables a day / in everything / not taking oneself / into account," and concludes:

someone
like that
is what I want
to be

Revered as a religious utterance, exploited in the 1940s as a wartime morale booster promoting self-sacrifice, and memorized by every subsequent generation of schoolchildren, "November 3rd" remains universally familiar in a way that no poem has been in the West since Kipling's "If" or Kilmer's "Trees." The world it evokes, a world of thatched huts and drought-stricken fields, sickly children and rice farmers with bent backs, might appear anachronistic when set against the Japan of computer graphics and advanced robot technology—unless you

---

Review of *A Future of Ice: Poems and Stories of a Japanese Buddhist* by Kenji Miyazawa, translated by Hiroaki Sato (Berkeley, CA: North Point Press, 1989). Reprinted from *VLS,* December 1989.

take a bus into the mountains and see landscapes and faces lifted intact from a Miyazawa poem.

In his own way Miyazawa came quite close to realizing the saintly ideal set forth in "November 3rd." The son of a pawnbroker in northern Japan's Iwate Prefecture (a backward region afflicted with chronic crop failures), he converted in adolescence to the Nichiren sect of Buddhism. Taking as his guide the *Lotus Sutra,* which teaches the availability of Buddhahood for all sentient beings, he dedicated himself to the welfare of the local farmers, becoming a sort of one-man cultural and agricultural missionary, teaching crop rotation and soil improvement and exploring methods of flood and drought prevention. In the meantime, as his translator notes, "he forced himself, unscientifically, to subsist on a poorer diet than even the local people were accustomed to, and ruined his health."

Such a career clearly lends itself to hagiography, and it is somewhat ironic that Miyazawa has been claimed in turn by militarists, Buddhists, modernist aesthetes, and most recently (so Gary Snyder tells us) the Japanese Greens. All these claims occurred after the poet was safely dead: for Miyazawa was not the sort of person ever to become a leader or spokesman. He was a strange mix of humility and irascibility, whimsy and anguish, and the self-imposed deprivations of his life contrast mysteriously with the exuberant profusion of his writing. His poems—he wrote several thousand, in both traditional and modern forms—range from epigrams to an eight-hundred-line free-verse notation of a journey on foot, from comic monologues to metaphysical reveries, from scientifically precise landscapes to fervent devotional outpourings, while his children's stories express sometimes surprisingly violent and tragic themes through a cast of animals, stars, and gods.

The scope and variety of Miyazawa's work is amply displayed in *A Future of Ice,* a revised and expanded follow-up to Hiroaki Sato's 1973 translation *Spring & Asura.* It forms part of a series of books (most of them, unfortunately, out of print) in which Sato has single-handedly set about making available the work of Japan's leading modern poets. The whole series is admirable, but this is the best of all, a full-scale portrait that clearly establishes Miyazawa as one of the most distinct poetic voices of this century. He was one of the most private as well. A single self-published collection in 1924 was his only gesture toward making his poetry public, his life was lived apart from literary circles, and—notwithstanding the vigorous modernity of his style—he thought of his writing more in religious than in aesthetic terms.

Miyazawa wrote at a time when Japanese poetry, after confining itself for a millennium or so to effusions of no more than thirty-three syllables, was branching out with gusto into the wide-open spaces of vers libre. But much of this work had a borrowed tone, heavy with Parnassian and Symbolist echoes, and imbued with a certain lugubrious self-pity. Miyazawa—for whom self-pity was never a mild emotion, but something closer to self-torture—nevertheless cultivated a bright, sharply defined, often comic diction, hurling incongruous elements together and letting them find their own unexpected unity.

Miyazawa gave the overall title *Spring & Asura* to all his poetry in modern forms. An *asura* is a demon, inhabiting one of the six Buddhist realms of existence, and the opposition of restless demon and vegetative landscape makes a fitting ideograph for Miyazawa's poetry, where consciousness erupts into its surroundings and mind does not merely contemplate the world but actively constructs it. Yet mind is also a construct:

> The phenomenon called "I"
> is a blue illumination
> of the hypothesized, organic alternating current lamp
>   (a compound of all transparent ghosts)
> a blue illumination
> of the karmic alternating current lamp
> which flickers busily, busily
> with landscapes, with everyone
> yet remains lit with such assuredness
>   (the light persists, the lamp lost).

Self, the organizing principle of consciousness, is fragmentary. The "I" of Miyazawa's diaristic voice charts its own disintegration into its compound elements: lava slopes, mineral deposits, parched reeds, foreign scientific terms, Sanskrit mantras, imaginary vistas of China or Italy or Russia, apparitions of Buddhist saints and demons, abstract patterns of line and color. (The expertise with which Miyazawa breaks down the world in his poems ties in curiously with his employment, in the last years of his life, as engineer for a local rock-crushing company.) The wonder is that this disintegration of self leads not into a void but into an ecstatic fullness: "Out of the gray steel of the imagination / akebi vines entwine the spider web, / wildrose bush, humus marsh," begins the title poem "Spring & Asura," one of Miyazawa's most energetic flights:

> At the bottom of the light in April's atmospheric strata,
> spitting, gnashing, pacing back and forth,
> I am Asura incarnate
> (the landscape sways in my tears)
> Shattered clouds to the limit of visibility
>   in heaven's sea of splendor
>   sacred crystalline winds sweep
>   spring's row of *Zypressen*
>   absorbs ether, black,
>   at its dark feet
>   the snow ridge of T'ien-shan glitters
>   (waves of heat haze & white polarization)
>   yet the True Words are lost
>   the clouds, torn, fly through the sky.

He is devotional but never didactic. Despite the orthodoxy of his religious beliefs, one never gets the feeling that Miyazawa is limiting himself to what he ought to say. On the contrary, there is a nakedness and spontaneity leading to constant surprise. In the poems concerning the death of his sister Toshiko in November 1922—including three written on the day itself—the grief is palpable and unpredictable in its manifestations. The death scene continues to well up in poems written the following year, along with visions of Toshiko assuming other forms: "Two large white birds fly / calling to each other sharply, sorrowfully / in the moist morning sunlight. / They are my sister, / my dead sister." Elsewhere, as the wheels of a train squeak noisily and a moth crawls under a ceiling lamp, he writes: "My feelings are warped with sorrow / and I can't help thinking of her, hidden somewhere."

In the wake of her death Miyazawa's poetry seems to toughen, mournful subjectivity hardening into mineral edge—"The sea is rusted by the morning's carbon dioxide"—and the poet taking a critical tone toward his own spiritual aspirations: "Why do you try to grasp firmly in the human / what is obtainable only in religion? / . . . Come now, wipe your tears, collect yourself. / You must not love in so religious a manner." Feeling, however intense, is not privileged over other levels of experience; it is a vehicle, not an end in itself. Many of Miyazawa's poems begin at a level of keyed-up emotion where someone else's would end, and extend a mood of turmoil in almost leisurely fashion, as if the poet were sufficiently at home in his own anxieties to feel out the space around them and take notes on the view.

His images suggest not so much the contents of his self as what remains after self has been exhausted. The world articulates itself in hard, jabbing lines: "The flock of crows is zinc scrap in dilute sulfuric acid." "Pale-blue sap oozes from the severed root." "The gray light avalanched in the distance." In the later poems the world enters more and more, bringing with it a varied population of animals (pigs, snakes, horses, insects) and humans whose doings are chronicled with almost novelistic density. A disheveled landlord, having loaned back the rice he's received as rent, goes off hunting to feed himself: "But when he manages to haul back a bear, / they say, 'He killed the mountain god / so this year's crop is poor.' " A young doctor begins to integrate himself into village life, and Miyazawa suddenly sees him as he will be in a few years: "By the time this doctor finally comes to feel / just as the villagers do . . . / he'll have fallen behind in new techniques / and at the lecture of the county doctor's society / he'll curl up small, a perpetual listener." The hallucinatory center of his poetry is framed by a broad, even humorous picture of the surrounding community. He is not apart from the world, but consciously alone in the midst of it, with all his senses operating.

The humor is chiefly evident in the monologues spoken by a series of bureaucratic or academic personae: "The Landscape Inspector," "Mr. Pamirs the Scholar Takes a Walk," "The Prefectural Engineer's Statement Regarding Clouds." Even in translation—or at least in translation as deft as Hiroaki Sato's—it is possible to gauge the juxtaposition of formulaic, ritually self-deprecating official language and the rugged, unresponsive landscape in whose midst it is spoken. Not surprisingly, the comedy has a bitter aftertaste, most memorably in "An Opinion Concerning a Proposed National Park Site," where the poet suggests turning his volcanic surroundings into a theme park embodying the Buddhist underworld:

> Now, set up a Hell here.
> Make it charming in the Oriental fashion.
> Put up a red fence of spears
> with a scattering of dead trees to terrify them . . .
> As a finale, blast off real shots electrically
> from two field cannons
> hidden this side of the mountain.
> The moment they think, Here we go!
> they'll find themselves in the real Styx.

In fact where he is—"this prefecture where there's nothing to eat"—is a lot tougher than Hell: "Over there on the frozen riverbed / a naked baby was found abandoned." The flights of fantastic invention always return to their source. What separates Miyazawa's poetry most strikingly from most of his modernist contemporaries in Europe and America is its immersion in actual hunger and actual labor. The imminence of drought or flood and the murderous difficulty of procuring sustenance can be felt in every line.

In the later poems, physical work is the abiding and obsessive theme, not work on behalf of some idealized nation-state or political program but for bare survival. The anguish is no longer metaphysical but practical: "I'm filled with anxieties about the manure / I threw from the horse cart and left on the slope yesterday." He monitors weather and growth as if vigilantly surveying the movements of a potential enemy: "I calculate again and again / the number of days before the delayed rice takes root, / the number of days before bifurcation, and the time when the ears will come out."

The real threat of starvation makes for the force of "The Breeze Comes Filling the Valley," a cry of triumph that, in the face of an anticipated crop failure and despite a violent flood of rain, "because of the slight differences in seedling preparation / and in the use of superphosphate, / all the stalks are up today." The triumph is only temporary, tentative—there will always be another season to worry about—but for the moment Miyazawa allows himself a moment of pure elation:

> I went home late at night.
> But in the end I did not sleep.
> And, look,
> this morning the east, the golden rose, opens,
> the clouds, the beacons, rise one after another,
> the high-voltage wires roar,
> the stagnant fog runs in the distance.
> The rice stalks have risen at last.
> They are living things,
> precision machines.
> All stand erect.
> At their tips, which waited patiently in the rain,
> tiny white flowers glisten
> and above the quiet amber puddles reflecting the sun
> red dragonflies glide.

This plenitude—literal, not metaphoric—is after all only another moment of reality, no more privileged than the others that Miyazawa recorded. Yet on the day of his death six years later, this tanka was the last poem he wrote: "Because of an illness, crumbling / this life— / if I could give it for ripening rice / how glad I would be."

Fusion Music

Kalidasa's *The Origin of the Young God*

The most exciting book of new poetry I've read lately is a translation of a sixteen-hundred-year-old Sanskrit epic. Hank Heifetz has had the audacity to take on a formally elaborate, densely allusive masterpiece in which rhythm, assonance, and wordplay are crucial—and the gift to make American poetry out of it. The poet and playwright Kalidasa (who wrote around A.D. 400) occupies a place comparable to Virgil or Dante in the Sanskrit poetic tradition, but that tradition's Western exposure has mostly been limited to departments of Indology. If he is known at all it's for his play *Sakuntala,* which when first translated in 1789 created a remarkable ripple effect among European writers. Despite that early impact, classical Indian literature has had nothing like the pervasive influence of Chinese and Japanese writing—chiefly because the translations have tended to suffer from what Heifetz calls "a tradition of the bad," a peculiar philological dialect equally remote from clear speech and graceful writing. *The Origin of the Young God* indicates just how much we have been missing.

At the poem's core is a fusion of sacred and profane. The plot describes a restoration of cosmic balance: a demonic Asura has gained control of the worlds, and can be defeated only by the child of the supreme god, Siva, and Parvati, daughter of the mountain-god Himalaya. To bring about the birth of this "young god," Parvati must distract Siva from his fearsome austerities.

Review of *The Origin of the Young God: Kalidasa's Kumarasambhava* translated and edited by Hank Heifetz (Berkeley and Los Angeles: University of California Press, 1985). Reprinted from *VLS,* November 1990.

Once various obstacles have been overcome (she wins him, in the end, by matching his own asceticism) the poem becomes a celebratory sequence of engagement, wedding, and sexual union.

But although all the characters are divine or superhuman, Kalidasa's metaphors speak a concrete and emotionally intimate language. We are simultaneously up among the gods and in the heart of earthly life: and the poet constantly reminds us that this double effect is made possible only by sublime tricks of image, rhythm, and rhetoric. He piles artifice on artifice: Parvati is "a collection of all things that are natural / similes for beauty," and her voice is so melodious that "even the song of the kokila / seemed harsh as a veena being played out of tune." The gods' temporary loss of dominance is likened to the way "the major rules of grammar / can be broken by exceptions."

Any visualization of a god must be illusory. To describe Siva is necessarily an exercise in contradiction: "The god who can be known in eight forms / fed wood to the fire, itself a form of him." Balletic flurries of paradox acknowledge the limit points where the divine escapes human formulation. But the divine is not merely elsewhere, it's also everywhere, so the terrifying and inconceivable Lord of life and death pays court and makes love like anyone else:

> How can others who are under the power of the senses
> stay unmoved when these emotions touch even the Lord?

Shuttling constantly between the impossible and the ordinary, Kalidasa creates a persistence of vision where the line between them blurs, and something like the unsayable gets said:

> Once it has come to touch that body, I know dust
> from the very ashes of the dead will purify the living,
> and so the gods smear their foreheads with it as it falls
> from the play of his limbs in the language of his dancing.

The winding arcs of the syntax balance eyelashes and galaxies. Heifetz brings across some of the linguistic qualities of Sanskrit through long wavelike constructions that test the carrying capacity of an English sentence:

> He blows into the hollows of bamboos with the wind
> rising up from the mouths of his caves as if he were
> sending that sound out as a drone note for demigod
> Kinnara musicians to build on when they sing.

From such distended loops of language he makes a persuasive music, deftly varied to suggest the original's interwoven meters.

That a work so ancient and remote should deliver such a jolt may say something about the condition of American poetry. Kalidasa's orchestrated lyricism seems almost too rich and ceremonious for our blood. He represents a poetry of perfected imagination, a poetry that lays out a luxuriant geography aswarm with lions and peacocks and wild boars whose "tusks seem as white as if / they had fed on sprouts of tender lotus stalks," and moves effortlessly between metaphysical abstractions and erotic particulars.

In accordance with the rules of its tradition, the poem suffuses each section with a particular "flavor," selected from a codified menu of emotions. In this suite of stylized feelings, every transitional nuance—sacred, erotic, comic, mournful, ornamental—is savored to its limit. The poem is at once an act of giving pleasure and a meditation on the ultimate nature of pleasure. Its rhythms describe a world of constant movement where every state is transient. Kalidasa's art arrests time's movement in order to display the beauty realized in that impossible pause:

> Seeming unable anymore to hold in
> the essence of the moonlight that it drinks while blooming,
> the lotus, suddenly releasing a humming
> of bees, bursts open down to its stem.

Voyage of Reconnaissance

Susan Howe

In 1982 I picked up a book called *Pythagorean Silence;* I had never heard of the author, Susan Howe, although she had already published five volumes of poetry. It was an unusual book to encounter at any time, and in the context of the early eighties the effect was otherworldly. In time Howe's writing would often be linked to the "language" poets, but there was an irreducible solitariness about her work: it didn't seem part of any conceivable group or school.

> Shapes   shadow-hunting
> Supremacy
>
> (cast now a shadow)
> Height of that tower diminished to
> this letter
> Light narrowed to this point or line
>
> Forfeit feeds nativity
>
> Ruin into rout
> Antiquity—   Runes
>
> a row of signs
> ordering sound
>
> (sacred and secret tree systems
> I sleep

Review of four books by Susan Howe: *Singularities* (Hanover, NH: Wesleyan University Press, 1990), *The Europe of Trusts* (Los Angeles: Sun and Moon Press, 1990), *A Bibliography of the King's Book or, Eikon Basilike* (Providence: Paradigm Press, 1989), and *My Emily Dickinson* (Berkeley, CA: North Atlantic Books, 1985). Reprinted from *VLS,* December 1990.

My initial impression was of movement: a world (was it ours?) in constant metamorphosis, a swirl of depths and tides, a series of transient landscapes (woods, seas, marshes) dissolving even as they were named. The aesthetic influences that came to mind were William Blake, Emily Brontë, Herman Melville, and beyond them echoes of all the poetry that came before. Yet a second look raised the question of where and how I perceived what I thought I was perceiving. Seen from a different angle, what was on the page showed up as a poetry of hard, dry clarity: spare, fragmented, analytical. Apparently nothing at all had been depicted or described.

It was an experience akin to getting a glimpse, in a Paul Klee painting, of a rich three-dimensional world and then, upon trying to locate it more precisely, coming up against a two-dimensional arrangement of shaded geometric forms that had shown, or pointed toward, something not there. The complex structures, images, and narratives Howe evoked were not actually written down; they existed in the margins of what was written down. The interior spaces I'd glimpsed were not in the words but in their unstated connections: in the decisiveness and freedom with which the words were laid side by side, and the abysses that were permitted to open up between them.

The freedom was most apparent in the use of words once possessed of tremendous power, but subsequently avoided by nearly all poets. For instance, there was a line reading in its entirety, "Broods infinity boundless": not one but three words of Miltonic bearing, and nothing but those words, jammed up against each other, surrounded by empty space, to produce a paradoxical effect of jagged disjunction. The notion of "boundless" was ripped from its context and plunked down to be looked at just as if it were any other word. Around the turn of the century poets had begun to abandon such words for any but ironic purposes because their meanings seemed used up. *Pythagorean Silence* did something quite different: tapping into the history of each word, as if there were hidden trails *inside* it that led toward still unexhausted half-lives.

Howe constructed a poetry in which each word was an actor, carrying its story with it, its chamber of echoes. In this disembodied drama, words talked about and acted on other words.

There was a forest of them; their interrelationships resembled a family or village. But abruptly, sometimes brutally, the solitariness of each was spelled out. At worst, the connections might exist only in the mind. For Howe this was only a starting point, the risk that all poetry runs. "Connections between unconnected things," she wrote in her study of Emily Dickinson, "are the unreal reality of poetry."

If the term *language poetry* meant anything at all, this surely was it. But unlike a good deal of work associated with that label, Howe's work affirmed connections as much as it questioned them. Her critical, demystifying intelligence was also capable of an unfamiliar, wild, oracular strain. The force of *Pythagorean Silence* came from an anguished doubleness of vision, where the same word might be both opening and closure, reality and disguise, truth and lie. The writing evoked a pain not localized but woven into all the reaches of human vocabulary, and perhaps most of all into words like *paradise* or *harmony* that posit a deliverance from pain.

In the years since, Howe has continued to produce work of a meditative urgency unmatched in recent American poetry. Her recent books make it clear that if she is a language poet she is also a history poet, charting discoveries and incursions, massacres and evasions, as they register in inherited texts. If her writing is at times as abstract as poetry can be, it is also as concrete as muskets fired in a wood or (in the mazelike, perpetually unverifiable scholarship she explores in *A Bibliography of the King's Book, or Eikon Basilike*) Charles I losing his head.

The Europe of Trusts (a collection bringing together *Pythagorean Silence, Defenestration of Prague,* and *The Liberties*) includes an introduction that illuminates the presence of history in Howe's poetry. "For me there was no silence before armies," she writes. Tracing her childhood from her birth in 1937, she charts the progress of war as it impinged on her consciousness, "a ship crowded with refugees" sailing from Ireland to America in 1938, her father enlisting after Pearl Harbor. "From 1939 until 1946 in news photographs, day after day I saw signs of culture exploding into murder. . . . If to see is to *have* at a distance, I had so many dead Innocents distance was abolished. . . . I became part of the ruin."

The poems in *The Europe of Trusts* (whose title pun yokes loyalties and financial combines) reach into what might be called the etymological unconscious. In an interview in the magazine *Talisman* Howe has stated: "Sounds and spirits (ghosts if you like) leave traces in a geography. . . . The tale and the place are tied in a mysterious and profound way." She studies runes, scratches, accretions of speech. Pieces of Europe—Iseult, Arthur, Socrates, Arden, Florimell, Proteus—rise momentarily to visibility like bits of wreckage in foam. Tiny phrases stand in for immense stories: "Mirror king of names cascading"—"Law chanted to the people from hills"—"Messenger / Drowned ship / Bright city."

She proceeds not by argument or description or chronological narrative but by tuning in to the deepest implications of her vocabulary. It's as if through the contemplation of words we could participate in what the historian Fernand Braudel called "long duration," the infinitesimally slow shifts in thought and feeling that take centuries or millennia rather than lifetimes. Sounded to its depths, the word *sky* leads back to eyes that are not ours looking at a sky that was not the same either. All history is present, all at once, striated like overlapping layers of mineral deposits, and punctuated by sudden chasms and faults.

Those chasms and faults could also be the lacunae and erasures of a written text, the obscure patches of a lost or mistranslated dialect. Increasingly Howe's poetry has confronted particular texts, working through them as if through a thicketed and problematic terrain. This stems in part from her long-term involvement with Emily Dickinson's work and the complex textual problems associated with it. Her critical study *My Emily Dickinson,* with its patient excavation of the vocabulary of a single poem, opens exciting possibilities not just for the reading of Dickinson but of poetry in general.

Howe restores an awareness of the immensity of a single word. A word has ancient roots, and its sphere of activity is potentially infinite. (In the *Talisman* interview she remarks, "Words are candles lighting the dark . . . . They reach up out there. A little flicker in silence . . . a signal.") The deceptively small proportions of a Dickinson poem gives way in her reading to an appreciation of hidden networks. The distance from one syllable to another can establish an epic scale.

Singularities (which incorporates the previously published *Articulation of Sound Forms in Time*) prompts a consideration of epic by the material it confronts: the Indian wars of New England, the American transformations and dilemmas to which Thoreau and Melville bear witness, the "settlement" of wilderness and its grotesque culmination in a devastated, commercialized Lake George: "In the seventeenth century European adventurer-traders burst through the forest to discover this particular long clear body of fresh water. They brought our story to it. Pathfinding believers in God and grammar spelled the lake into *place*."

Language takes land captive. Thought can only think with what has already been named. Hence her preoccupation with nouns and even more so with proper nouns. Names change, are assumed, split into variants. A name is not a fixed entity but the description of a process. No linguistic activity is more insistent than naming in its staking out of the real. The work called "Thorow" is involved with the writings of Thoreau; the title is a misspelling that occurs in a letter by Hawthorne; it is also an obsolete spelling of *through*. Howe has stated that her purpose was "to go *through* the name, to open it up." Or, as the poem says: "We go through the word Forest."

We go through it, or it goes through us. The story is inside us, or we are inside the story. The unease of language—the chafing of thought against the means of its own articulation—lies in our inability to stand outside it, to dominate it. The "master stories" of conquest and progress try to invent controllable sentences. Howe's description of her own approach is distinctly different: "I write to break out into perfect primeval Consent."

Would that consent be the threshold beyond which language can melt away from history? But history—the world—is everywhere, in every syllable: in the very syllables that aspire toward an impossible freedom. "Blind destiny menacing catastrophe": a teleological dread informs her lines at times, a sense of time rushing toward disaster. All the doctrines imprinted at one time or another in language—all notions of order, harmony, center, authority, tradition, law—come out in the poetry, but they are set adrift, scattered, disarranged. The encounter with the world is by its nature unfinished. Poetry is rapid—"fixed in fleeting"—because it must be to travel at the speed of meaning. At the point of contact (and nothing is harder than to stay there) everything starts fresh: "I thought I stood on the shores of a history of the world where forms of wildness brought up by memory become desire and multiply . . . Interior assembling of forces underneath earth's eye. Yes, she, the Strange, excluded from formalism. I heard poems inhabited by voices."

The Mayakovsky of Macdougal Street

Frank O'Hara

Side by side with an extract from *Leaves of Grass,* a line of Frank O'Hara's adorns the railing along the esplanade of New York's Battery Park City: "One need never leave the confines of New York to get all the greenery one wishes—I can't even enjoy a blade of grass unless I know there's a subway handy, or a record store or some other sign that people do not totally *regret* life." Actually, the line (from "Meditations in an Emergency") is misquoted: the italics have been dropped, with their suggestion of live speech caught in passing.

One wonders what O'Hara would have made of this bit of graven immortality. He would certainly have approved of being paired with Whitman (whom he invoked as "my great predecessor") and with his eye for city views might well have savored the setting's incongruous juxtaposition of sea and crowds and corporate architecture, gawking tourists and roller-blading youth against a backdrop of hundred-foot yachts with names like *This Is It* and *Pleasant Moments,* the old-fashioned red-and-white Colgate sign on the Jersey side of the water facing off the sleek postmodern kitschiness of the palm court of the World Financial Center.

On the other hand, the contemporary panorama might have struck him as unexpectedly sterile and dispirited, a more cowed and anonymous spectacle than the New York of which his poems have become both emblem and repository, the New York of

---

Review of *City Poet: The Life and Times of Frank O'Hara* by Brad Gooch (New York: Alfred A. Knopf, 1993). Reprinted from *New York Review of Books,* December 2, 1993.

Pollock and Balanchine and Billie Holiday, the Cedar Tavern and the Five Spot and the Roxy, when artists were artists, parties were parties, and record stores tended to be more cozy and idiosyncratic than those in the shadow of the Financial Center.

There is no escaping the nostalgia that pervades any consideration of O'Hara's life and writing, a nostalgia he helped invent with his mythologizing of his social life. (In a letter to James Schuyler, he wrote, "I make 'real life' into a fantasy which bears little resemblance to the actual and largely fortuitous events which inspired it in the first place.") Do we respond most in reading him to a generic sense of dailiness, or to the evocation of a golden era imagined to have occurred roughly between 1951 and 1965? (That era's liveliness was of course not all imagination. Consider Brad Gooch's list of the regulars at the San Remo bar in Greenwich Village, only one of many such clusters: "Tennessee Williams, John Cage, Paul Goodman, Dylan Thomas, Allen Ginsberg, William Burroughs, Judith Malina and Julian Beck, Miles Davis, Merce Cunningham, Dorothy Day, and James Agee.")

Allen Ginsberg said of O'Hara's New York poems, "It's like having Catullus change your view of the Forum in Rome," and indeed one has to go back to fairly remote periods—ancient Rome, eighteenth-century London—to find poetry as meticulous in its gossip and as minute in its urban observation as O'Hara's. He made himself the patron poet of a this-worldly magic emanating chiefly from the magic city of New York: a utopia of freely circulating desire articulated by sex, talk, drink, art, ballet, parties, movies, and lunch dates, with occasional necessary forays to the Hamptons and Paris. The poems take their place as evidence toward that taxonomy of partying which would be a prerequisite for a thoroughgoing social history of the American fifties and sixties, and in which the genus *O'Hara* would have to be clearly distinguished from the varieties associated with Capote, Warhol, or Kesey.

For O'Hara the contemplation of a bright bubble world was at the heart of his deepest concerns: to protect the fragility of pleasure, to extend the live moment without embalming it, to create through poetry a space for perfect liberty, unbridled whim. He welcomes whatever is incomplete, interrupted, unplanned: anything that contradicts the orderly completeness of death. On all occasions he is ready to toss in the little life-affirming asides that serve as something of a vamp for his free-associating riffs: "the Pittsburgh pirates shout because they won / and in a sense we're all winning / we're alive" ("Steps") or "it's also pretty hard to remember life's marvellous / but there it is guttering choking then soaring / in the mirrored room of this consciousness" ("In Favor of One's Time") or "the only thing to do is simply continue / is that simple / yes, it is simple because it is the only thing to do" ("Adieu to Norman, Bon Jour to Joan and Jean-Paul").

Decades of echoes and imitations have somewhat blurred the singularity of encountering Frank O'Hara's poetry in its time. I first came across his work in Donald Allen's anthology *The New American Poetry: 1945–1960* and can remember how absolutely distinct a sound O'Hara made even in such noisy and variegated company as Charles Olson, Allen Ginsberg, LeRoi Jones, Gary Snyder, Jack Spicer, and Michael McClure. The Allen anthology (for which, we learn from Brad Gooch's biography, O'Hara served as "primary unofficial consultant") was uniquely influential in establishing the notion of a generational wave of innovation taking its inspiration from abstract expressionism and jazz, yet O'Hara's work seemed removed from any strong affiliation to a poetic, political, or spiritual school. Its casual directness and unapologetic ebullience undercut millennia of pedagogical solemnity, and made other poetry—including that of his Beat and Black Mountain contemporaries—seem a bit pompous and portentous by comparison.

First of all it was funny, funny enough to get a laugh from readers without much interest in contemporary verse. The humor lay in capturing the disjunctions and intrusions of actual, as opposed to ideal, thought processes. It was as if he tape-recorded his brain at work and then played the most startling moments back for the amusement of his friends. Nothing was unthinkable or unsayable; he was so at home in his emotional disorder that even the depths of anxiety assumed a certain pastoral charm.

The flavoring of the jolt might be mock-grand—"All things

are tragic when a mother watches!"—or nasty-hip—"a lady asks us for a nickel for a terrible / disease but we don't give her one we / we don't like terrible diseases"—or silly-confessional—

> I have a drink,
> it doesn't help—far from it!
> I
> feel worse. I can't remember how
> I felt, so perhaps I feel better.

—or raucously goofy:

> YIPPEE! I'm glad I'm alive
> "I'm glad you're alive
> too, baby, because I want to fuck you"

There was the impression of a whole world there, not transfigured but literally dragged in, papaya juice and *Forbidden Planet,* genitals and clouds, Pasternak and Madison Avenue. He acknowledged how much poetry had to compete with in order to register as real pleasure or real experience at all: "And after all, only Whitman and Crane and Williams, of the American poets, are better than the movies." It took courage to remind the reader so insistently of all the other things he could be doing—making love or going for a walk or throwing a party. To someone who half-suspected that he would really rather be watching *Northern Pursuit* on television, O'Hara confided that he'd rather be doing that too. His poetry existed not as a distraction from the noise of the world but as a conscious part of it. He meant to be read as he wrote: almost drowned out by all the other voices, somehow penetrating an urban fog of honks and clinks.

O'Hara's formative poetic taste was for the French modernist dislocations of Apollinaire, Reverdy, Jacob, Desnos, and others (an influence that for all its promise of unlimited freedom weighs a little ponderously in some of his earlier work), but he tempered those imported sounds with the American accent and abrupt manners of William Carlos Williams, Vladimir Mayakovsky's flair for free-form harangue, and his own finely tuned ear for the patterns of conversation floating around him in

Manhattan. Clearly these fusions were the product of a long and laborious process, but it was O'Hara's virtuoso trick to make it appear an invention of the moment.

That he could write so well so fast undoubtedly owes much to the discipline he absorbed through years as an aspiring composer and concert pianist. Curiously, considering how much his career was associated with poetry and sculpture, music seems to have provided the deepest impetus. After the names and incidents drop away, his poems can be read as abstract constructions modeled on the works of his early heroes: Stravinsky, Hindemith, Honegger, Prokofiev, Milhaud, Copland—not to mention Rachmaninoff, to whom he dedicated a string of birthday poems. As he wrote in the autobiographical "Ode to Michael Goldberg('s Birth and Other Births)":

> the wind sounded exactly like
> Stravinsky
>   I first recognized art
> as wildness, and it seemed right,
>   I mean rite, to me

O'Hara's brand of spontaneity was anything but simple. Its sincerity was mixed with an equal blend of acknowledged insincerity; it made room for splenetic outbursts and seductive asides, cries of faux-naïf wonderment, fragments of needling conversation and campy banter, breathless cataloging of local gossip ("Joe has a cold and is not coming to Kenneth's / although he is coming to lunch with Norman"), midtown street scenes ("who dropped that empty carton / of cracker jacks"), and old movies ("Miriam Hopkins dropping her champagne glass off Joel McCrea's yacht / and crying into the dappled sea").

The effect was very much of having an intimate acquaintance ring up, a little crocked, and murmur a stream of amusing, insinuating comments that led unexpectedly into the jab of a home truth ("don't be shy of unkindness, either / it's cleansing and allows you to be direct / like an arrow that feels something") or self-revelation ("I drink to reduce my seriousness so a certain spurious charm can appear"). And on top of that he could stand back and describe what he was doing as if he were talking about someone else:

> I'm not going to cry all the time
> nor shall I laugh all the time,
> I don't prefer one "strain" to another.
> I'd have the immediacy of a bad movie,
> not just a sleeper, but also the big,
> overproduced first-run kind. I want to be
> at least as alive as the vulgar. And if
> some aficionado of my mess says "That's
> not like Frank!", all to the good!
>
> ("My Heart")

The poems didn't represent life; they seemed part of it. Like the tankas exchanged by the ancient Japanese courtiers of *The Tale of Genji,* O'Hara's lyrics were mechanisms making something happen in life, actions rather than artifacts. Their beauty was of a random scattering whose messiness turns out—as if by accident—to be laid out with an exquisite eye for form.

O'Hara's most successful trick—an enduring one—was to make any reader believe that he knew him personally. In a letter written to the painter Fairfield Porter in 1955—a letter whose self-deprecating tone is too lovingly elaborated to be quite convincing—he described his poetry as "full of objects for their own sake, spleen and ironically intimate observation which may be truthfulness (in the lyrical sense) but is more likely to be egotistical cynicism masquerading as honesty. . . . Where Kenneth [Koch] and Jimmy [Schuyler] produce art, for instance, I often feel I just produce the by-product of exhibitionism. Well, chacun à son mauvais goût!" Elsewhere, in the brilliant and comic manifesto "Personism," he put the matter rather differently: "It does not have to do with personality or intimacy, far from it!"

Brad Gooch's biography *City Poet* has all the gossipy and glamorous pleasures usually associated with celebrity bios, pleasures rarely found in accounts of the lives of modern American poets. There are no visions, dementia, or suicide here; little solitude of any sort, in fact. The poet figures as part of a particularly brilliant crowd—or perhaps as its secret orchestrator. It is a disconcertingly jaunty chronicle, even as its central character winds down with a shrug of inevitability into too much alcohol and hints of exhaustion.

The lines are outwardly simple. Small-town Catholic upbringing, early musical training, a World War II stint in the navy (he was present at the Japanese surrender) that seems to have enabled him to sever his ties to home, four years at Harvard during which his focus switched from music to poetry, and where he first met John Ashbery; graduate work and a prestigious poetry prize at the University of Michigan; and thereafter pretty much the New York whirl, as he worked his way up the ladder at the Museum of Modern Art (by the time of his death he was an associate curator) and became part of that extravagant company of painters and poets including Larry Rivers, Jane Freilicher, Grace Hartigan, Willem de Kooning, Kenneth Koch, and James Schuyler. He was cut off at forty, as he stumbled in the dark into the path of a dune buggy on Fire Island; Gooch suggests that he might have survived had his liver not already been weakened by years of hard drinking. In the interstices of that life the poetry somehow got written, much of it scattered in letters and one-off copies and smeared notes strewn around his own and others' apartments.

The revelation here is the O'Hara we don't really get to meet in his poetry, the earnest youth he more or less discarded, and who emerges as a remarkably appealing character and, not surprisingly, a surpassingly articulate one. Gooch charts O'Hara's early development largely in his own words: in the letters he wrote home from the navy, for instance, he comes across as serious, self-reliant, and straightforward, with an altogether unironic appreciation of being alive.

His advice to his parents on how to listen to Brahms' Violin Concerto—"Be sure & notice in the Finale how the theme (main) begins (start of the 8th record I think) and then recurs about twice as fast, or perhaps just with a different emphasis (about ½ way thru the 9th record I think)"—foreshadows his poems' serpentine shifts of tone and tempo. The endearing accents of a hometown kid, as he berates the Southerners in his barracks for being "so darn anti-Negro" and relays his enthusiasm for Marlene Dietrich in *Kismet* ("Was she exotic"), give way to a calm self-awareness as he writes from overseas: "Except for swimming, most of my real pleasures are in my mind. So are always at my fingertips."

When his naval stint ends (he served on a destroyer as a sonarman third class) a transformation becomes evident in a series of striking letters to his parents in which he begins to discard his inherited cultural baggage. "Our religion rather encourages us," he writes, "to picture death as a relief and a refuge, it seems to me as I think of it; and I can't help but think that that is not healthy and wholesome. . . . why prefer the shadow to the sunlight, water to land?" He quarrels with what he saw as Catholicism's rejection of the world, retorting: "It is our natural habitat and is not rejection of it cowardice or laziness of one kind or another?"

By the time he is back in the States, he is ready to cut his ties. In a letter that (although he makes no open acknowledgment of his homosexuality) is remarkable for its assured candor, he declares: "It's independence I want. There are things I must learn for myself and undoubtedly they will hurt—but not forever. I'd rather be hurt than stunted anyhow. And besides—perhaps the worst has already happened! It hasn't killed me yet. Very few things will shock me, I'm afraid." From the time he got out of the navy, O'Hara lived with the urgency of someone aware of precisely how much he has to do in the time allotted to him. In a journal he kept at Harvard in 1948 he wrote, "One must hurry, one must avoid impediments, snares, detours; one must not be stifled in a closed social or artistic railway station waiting for the train; I've a long way to go, and I'm late already."

We don't, in Gooch's account, get any closer to O'Hara than in these early letters and journals. It may be that he was too much the annotator of his own life to allow much space for anyone else to assume that role: or simply that there is less private life to be explored in a life lived relentlessly in company. It was his show, a show so exhilarating that most of his friends seem to have been happy to give plenty of leeway to the contradictions of someone for whom the paths of desire were almost voluntarily complex.

The resulting web of passionate, frequently unresolved sexual and emotional entanglements provides Gooch with his richest material as he parses the intricacies of O'Hara's involvements with men gay and straight, and with a succession of women—V. R. Lang, Jane Freilicher, Grace Hartigan, and others—who figure in a muselike role in much of his poetry. It did not make things simpler for him that, in Gooch's words, "his ultimate dream lover was clearly a straight painter." (While spending time in Madrid he wrote characteristically that it was "just like New York in that one has the same kind of relationships here. . . . That is, the queens always hate me and the heterosexual painters seem to like me.")

Whenever his liaisons threaten to veer into Dostoyevskian intensity—in the accounts, for example, of his tempestuous involvement with Larry Rivers—a note of comedy frequently intervenes, as in the account of one would-be lover of O'Hara's (another straight painter): "It was a fiasco. . . . Both of us started to laugh at the same time." O'Hara was able to make that kind of what-the-hell laughter part of his poetry, at a time when literary homosexuality was generally surrounded by an aura of obligatory anxiety and self-doubt.

Everyone who knew O'Hara seems eager to talk about him at length, and the mingling of their testimony creates the impression of a wake still, after all these years, in progress. If O'Hara was absorbed by his own charm, he was not alone. Willem de Kooning said of his advent among the painters, "Right away he was at the center of things, and he did not bulldoze. There was a good-omen feeling about him." Larry Rivers's comment is typical: "Frank was just a joy to be with. He was smart on any subject. Anything you said he had like five responses and you were throwing the ideas against a fantastic wall and it would come back more brilliant than you had ever intended it." He played the same incandescent role for the poets of what became known as the New York School.

Gooch delineates the social currents of O'Hara's life skillfully and entertainingly; he is less informative when it comes to the poetic milieu in which O'Hara operated. Analyses of style are too vague to be of any use: we are told that "the New York School could be grouped together because they wrote in language that was illogical and often meaningless," John Ashbery's poetry is described as "a record of whatever thoughts, memories, or words were in his mind at a given time," and John Wieners's work is characterized not very helpfully in terms of "visionary exaggerations" and "darkly 'beat' personal style." Passing errors—like confusing Robert Kelly with Robert Creeley in a discussion of "deep image" poetry—betray a certain casualness with regard to the nuances of a world in which O'Hara was a supremely sophisticated participant.

Any biography of O'Hara must be an uncompleted arc. He died not precisely at his peak—poetry had been on the wane for several years, the always heavy drinking was taking a more visible toll—but at thirty-nine he had hardly exhausted his opportunities. He was on the brink of a wider literary fame and his rising curatorial career was giving him an ever more influential role in the art world. At the same time he defined his own moment so precisely that it is hard to imagine him in a subsequent era. By the time of his death he was already ill at ease with much that would become typical of sixties culture; mystical religiosity and political conformity of any stripe were alike inimical to him. The pugnacious vivacity of his temperament might have found the subsequent decades a trying experience.

John Ashbery, responding to O'Hara's use of personal references in his poetry, commented: "The fact that no one would know who the people are would add rather than decrease charm." It remains a question how much *City Poet*'s gloss on the social and romantic occasions of the poems really changes their effect. How much did we need to know about who Jane and Vincent and Patsy and Mike and Joe were when they weren't being syllables in a poem? Surprisingly little, I think. We could have guessed most of it, not from information that the poems impart, but from the almost imperceptible shifts of emotion and humor they trace with such uncanny precision. In a poem like "How to Get There" the network of human relations—"lies, lies everywhere writhing and gasping, clutching and tangling"—becomes an abstract space in which the poet stages an elegant disappearing act:

> never to be alone again
> never to be loved
> sailing through space : didn't I have you once for my self?
> West Side?
> for a couple of hours, but I am not that person

It was appropriate that one of his very best poems be entitled "In Memory of My Feelings": it was his faithfulness to the real messiness and fluidity of feeling that made O'Hara so much more than the Surrealist pasticheur he might have become.

The paradox at the heart of his writing is a sort of disinterested self-absorption. He does not so much transcend the graspings of desire as inhabit them so fully that he achieves an affectionate parody of a petulant and ennui-ridden egoism: "I am the least difficult of men. All I want is boundless love" ("Meditations in an Emergency") or

> I am terribly bored
> sometimes it is like seeing a bad movie
> other days, more often, it's like having an acute disease of the
> kidney
> god knows it has nothing to do with the heart
> nothing to do with people more interesting than myself
> yak yak
> that's an amusing thought
> how can anyone be more amusing than oneself
> how can anyone fail to be
>
> ("Yesterday Down at the Canal")

The graph of this self-absorption becomes, in a brilliant poetic sleight of hand, the mirror of a world. In the solitude in which he is never alone, O'Hara turns his mind into a theater where the crisscrossing dialogues never end. Everything talks back to him, even the sun. The least hermetic of poets, he can afford to look in the mirror because he sees everything reflected there anyway:

> Now I am quietly waiting for
> the catastrophe of my personality
> to seem beautiful again,
> and interesting, and modern.
>
> ("Mayakovsky")

Most of the time it was all of that.

Song, Scream, Fountain

Jerome Rothenberg

With Jerome Rothenberg's *Gematria* following closely on his *Lorca Variations,* it's a good season for thinking again about a poet whose influence is as pervasive as it is infrequently acknowledged—and for thinking of Rothenberg above all as poet rather than as editor, translator, commentator, or performer. If Rothenberg's poetry isn't talked about as often as it ought to be, it is in part because he himself has suggested so many other topics. A discussion of his work is apt to lead away from it, along any of the branching pathways he has opened, into a conversation about ethnopoetics or aleatory composition or Yaqui song forms, Poland or Dada or Kabbalah.

As anthologist—in the series of collections ranging from *Technicians of the Sacred* (1968), the poetic *Whole Earth Catalogue* of its day, to *Exiled in the Word* (1989), his idiosyncratic reshuffling of Jewish tradition—he has aspired toward maximum inclusiveness, seeking not to delimit the areas he focused on but to extend them, to reveal multiple voices and secret correspondences already hidden in them. By equating archaic and experimental, primitive and complex, he offered contemporary poets an opportunity to conceive of their roots as deeper and wider than any narrowly defined academic lineage.

No poet has been more explicit about his own influences. The titles and dedications of his poems are a map of sources and relations: Lorca, Celan, Tristan Tzara, Kurt Schwitters, Gertrude Stein, Arshile Gorky. Likewise, few poets have articulated quite

---

Review of *Gematria* by Jerome Rothenberg (Los Angeles: Sun and Moon Press, 1994). Reprinted from *VLS,* December 1994.

so precisely their aims and methods. This can have its disadvantages; we run the risk of not seeing the poem for the program. To look at his poetry apart even from the context he has created for it is to allow free rein to the sense of the uncanny, the power of strangeness. "I have no desire to work in isolation & I don't," he has written, yet the power of his poetry is precisely in its acknowledgment of an isolation that is nexus of both prophecy and terror.

The outer trappings—the cloaks, masks, jargons, rites, story lines, codes of identity—are set in motion with a magician's flair for unanticipated transformations. Their inner workings, the rhythms of that motion and the grammar of those transformations, are harder to discern. Putting everything on the table may be the best way for the poet to guard his secrets.

A drama of revelation is enacted over and over: what was hidden is revealed, but by the same token what is visible remains in some sense hidden. The world opens wide into mystery; the clarity of language brings us ever more intimately into the presence of an unrelenting obscurity, a permanent and sacred darkness. The question posed toward the end of Rothenberg's early sequence *The Seven Hells of the Jigoku Zoshi* (1962)—"The mind of man is on fire / And where will his eye find rest"—suggests the impetus behind the process of image-generation he continually enacts.

In *The Seven Hells* he had already demonstrated the possibility of extended lyrical narrative, a scroll-poem fusing image and episode, story line and poetic line. The "deep image" by which he defined his earliest poetics was something like a compressed history, rendered in a vernacular stylized into cragginess. This impulse found its culmination in those long poems whose accretion of details have built up a world—shtetl or lager, shaman's forest or hallucinatory city—with almost novelistic density. *Poland/1931* (1974) and *Khurbn* (1989) reclaim for poetry a narrational power elsewhere mostly conceded to fiction or history. The long poems increasingly have seemed designed for public recitation, suggesting a reinvention of poetic drama already implicit in *The Seven Hells,* which did not so much describe a mythic underworld as act it out.

In that kind of choric poetry it is possible to confuse reciting voice and recited text, or to see the text as a libretto not fully realized until delivered before an audience. Some who have attended Rothenberg's readings may well think of him primarily as a performance poet, for whom the timing and intensity of vocal delivery are as crucial as the words themselves.

But poised against that there has always been what might be called his runic or totemic mode: the concentrated abstraction evident in such early sequences as *Sightings* and *The Gorky Poems,* whether in the textured layers of "Charred Beloved"—

> Fire night.
> Falling.
> In threes.
> Winter weather.
> Sand's eye.
> Heaven.
> Makes a place for it.
> Sea comb.
> Hard.
> Webs of tears for it.

—or the minimalist units of "Cages," a series of single words set off by white space and the repeating title, culminating neatly in:

> *Cages (7)*
> Cages.

Here the field of language can be visualized as a bare yard demarcated by irregular pieces of sculpture, a yard whose blank spaces are as significant as the objects that interrupt them. Those white expanses serve to emphasize how very rough-hewn and awkward are the chunks of language strewn in their midst.

The presence of the word imposes a sense of oddity that merges with a suggestion of awe that anything at all should be present. Not that meanings are cut loose or set aside, but that priority of attention is given to the physical means by which meaning is apprehended, the word existing before and beyond meaning. In this light it should be recalled that it was in Rothenberg's magazine of ethnopoetics, *Alcheringa,* that language poetry first received major attention.

In *Gematria* Rothenberg strips his poetry down as if he wished to insist, this time out, on how many components can be removed before getting to the ones that are quite essential. Every poet dreams of reducing the art to its elements, of laying out the materials as on a workshop table, to expose what poems are made of without any need to explain or even combine. The satisfactions of *Gematria* are of getting at the marrow of a poetic intent without impediment or ornamental shrubbery, of arriving at a place where there is no room for anything but the poem, which by now may consist of only two or three words—

AN INHERITANCE
Shut—
like the rain.

or perhaps only one:

EVENING
Evil.

The form is ancient, a Jewish numerological method based on the assignment of numerical value to Hebrew letters and on the principle that words of equal value are linked in meaning. Eventually the technique was adopted for increasingly elaborate esoteric purposes. In the Kabbalah of the Names expounded by the thirteenth-century mystic Abraham Abulafia, the letters of the Hebrew alphabet are both a conduit to ecstatic experience and a means to grasp the inner meaning of Torah. Alphabet as the matrix by means of which the universe came into being, scripture as encryption of a hidden intellectual universe: these are among the more dizzying conceptions of the hermeneutic tradition that (according to Rothenberg's explication in *Exiled in the Word*) used the technique of *gematria* "to discover divine & angelic names & to uncover correspondences between ideas & images by means free of subjective interference."

Rothenberg, however, disavows any such explicitly religious intent; the word associations, although based on the numerical values of vocabulary of the Torah, are to lead away from any enclosing system into the country of surprise. Yet the evocation of such a spiritual possibility imparts its flavor to the whole project, as it has to earlier poems, the one from *The Notebooks* in which the Alphabet appears in a dream ("& I thought / 'you are numbers first before you are sound") or the dance of letters in *Abulafia's Circles:* "red alephs / yellow yods / blue hum of ayins."

In *Gematria* narrative is in the gaps between words. A true concrete poetry, it allows the oppressive power of words to be felt—and at the same time lifts the burden by shifting it outward, into plain sight. The mightiest forces, the most ancient histories are made miniature. The reader holds in his hand a lexicon of the world: steal, rock, hats, rings, emptied, tree, blood, tail, perish, foreskin, household, spices, birds, walking, deaf, midnight. Words are placed in one another's neighborhood so that their respective powers act upon each other: light and stranger, song and scream, fountain and eye, God and blemish, dominion and parable. The equations are neither simple nor utterly opaque. The influences brought to bear on each other have multiple and unexpected consequences: as Rothenberg wrote years ago in *The Gorky Poems,* "Perhaps it is always those things that can't be *really* defined that are the most interesting elements in any relationship. A matter of convergence."

The poetic whose bare bones are revealed by this process of emptying out is anything but desiccated. A life teems in these spaces, a life of fear and wilderness, of calf and jasmine and dream. I can imagine walking through a labyrinthine building of which these words would be the walls: or rather, in reading *Gematria* I do walk through such a building and find it an unexpected and constantly changing house of language.

Merrill's Poe

To James Merrill I owe an indelible experience of poetry read aloud. At a marathon tribute to John Hollander's anthology of nineteenth-century American poetry, he reduced a large crowd to uncanny silence with his reading of that most overfamiliar of poems, Edgar Allan Poe's "Annabel Lee." From the first syllables it was apparent that he was exploring unsuspected metrical and tonal reaches of lines that most interpreters—for want of perceiving any other option—would have reduced to doggerel. The precision of his accents and the melodic range of his voicings revealed (or did they invent?) an extraordinary and unsuspected poem, as subtle and many-layered as a Monteverdi madrigal, a hall of surflike assonances through which floated phrases that suddenly and unaccountably were made to seem freshly born—"she was a *child*" and "the angels not half so happy in Heaven" and "so, all the night-tide." Merrill's revivifying of a poem usually unhearable demonstrated in remarkable fashion the power of the poetic ear to make new. He heard and gave voice to what he heard and it was as if he had brought a different poem into being on the spot—the poem as it might have sounded when it was still inside Poe's head.

Reprinted from *Village Voice,* February 21, 1995.

Life with All the Repeats

Michael O'Brien

"Too many poems are demonstrations of cultural adequacy, a kind of showing your license to the poetry cop who has just pulled your sports car over to the side of the road. It's very liberating to realize that no one is watching, no one gives a fuck. Once you stop feeling sorry for yourself you realize that it leaves you absolutely free. You can do what you want."

I'm talking to Michael O'Brien about his new book *The Floor and the Breath,* renewing a conversation about poetry that we have been carrying on for several decades now, a conversation punctuated by the pleasure of hearing his judiciously modulated readings of his own work. During that time a series of books have appeared at all too infrequent intervals: *The Summer Poems* (1967), *Blue Springs* (1976), *Conversations at the West End* (1979), the twin volumes *Veil, Hard Rain* and *The Ruin* (1986). They have not, apparently, spoken vociferously enough to receive much of what passes (by the minimal standards of the day) for critical attention. The irony is that Michael O'Brien's order of lyric intelligence embodies qualities—of emotional directness, musical subtlety, and worldly perception—for which I suspect many readers of poetry are starved.

His triumph is to have turned relative neglect into an occasion for liberation. I don't know any poet who goes his own way with a more deliberate self-assurance. The results can be seen in all his writing, but most especially in *The Floor and the Breath,* whose astringent lyricism cuts effortlessly through the ambient

---

Review of *The Floor and the Breath* by Michael O'Brien (New York: Cairn Editions, 1995). Reprinted from *VLS,* June 1995.

smoke and hubbub. Here is a book that has the world in it, the world of New York, the world of snow and luggage and plastic bags, of aspirin and bare sky: "life with all the repeats, cradled in space, a chorus, indelible." Yet for all its gritty engagement with the thing-ness of things, it's also a book shaped by an unrelenting sense of abstraction. O'Brien's attentiveness is needle-thin and needle-sharp.

To talk with him about his poetry is to talk about music, cadence, dance: "There's a kind of dance of attenuation and abundance that the poems try not to conclude. Their life has to do with that tension too, the oscillation between those possibilities." If he talks about a certain "meagerness of experience," it's a meagerness that carries within it a treasury of potential detail. The "blue steady trembling of a welder's flame," "the wave's black hollow," the "mirror-writing / of a bus's windows": this vocabulary of discrete perceptions, built up over years of patient notation, provides the means for acknowledging a "virtuosity / of space" otherwise beyond articulation.

Similes are basic to this poetry: "It's very involuntary, it's very much a way the world is first given to me." They are everywhere: radio static is "a sound like the sugaring of marble," "New York's iron snow is worn as a sink," "four men stand like empties outside the Stanley Employment Agency." The precision of the notation is remarkable in itself, enough so for a single detail to constitute the whole: in a brief poem about an elevator, the way a woman's leather jacket "creaks like a mast" becomes, through the exact evocation of sound effect and enclosed site, a self-sufficient embodiment of the claustrophobia of desire.

To make a record of such particulars has been a familiar task to poets as disparate as Horace and Hitomaro and the anonymous maker of the Exeter Book of Riddles, a task disdained by some contemporaries who find the mere registering of earthly phenomena insufficient occasion for poetry. O'Brien has consciously resisted the temptation to "work up" a poem from its perceptual starting point, as if the materials of the world were merely counters in some larger philosophical or political schema. It's enough at times simply to define what a radio is, or a translation, or an echocardiogram.

In this light he remarks about traditional Japanese poetics:

"The isolation of the individual unit of perception is very attractive to me, the sense of its sufficiency: that spectacles are not to be moralized. . . . The imagists, like the Japanese, had that sense that you didn't have to work up a poem; and you can see people doing that today, starting a poem with a kind of image or construct that could be left by itself as the poem, and the poet deciding to take it further. I've always been of two minds about the wisdom of that choice."

But O'Brien is doing more than compiling a daybook of textures and sensations, a dictionary of sensory correspondences. Every passing resemblance, every recurrence of the word *like* (and it kicks in often enough to serve as a kind of offbeat rhythm section, a quick crash of cymbal to punctuate the flow) carries an implication of fracture. There is always the possibility that a simile is nothing more than an invention raised in the face of irreparable unlikeness. Within the profusion of similes lurks a fundamental disbelief that anything can really be *like* another thing:

> Seeming is rhyming
> but finally
> things rhyme only with themselves.

Both terms of the simile's equation are adrift in the world, flung down side by side, but not necessarily evidence of any underlying or transcending order:

> The world and its likeness
> given at once
>
> The world and the world
>
> It is not a selection

The objects set against each other touch off cascades of mirror images—"I turn from the sunset / and find it reflected in an idler's dark glasses"—in the same way that words in random collision elicit flurries of puns and echoes.

For all the filigree and arabesque of these disturbances in the field of perception, a starkness persists. O'Brien writes, he says, from a sense that "reality is both particular and impoverished in some way." But impoverishment is not emptiness; nor is it stasis. For a book that more or less eschews linear narrative, *The Floor and the Breath* swarms with stories, and with the spaces in which stories might occur: "Six in the evening, August, a bar on Barrow, door open to the street, Christmas lights, a horse race on TV." A life can be told in a handful of words: "One day, homesick for the body, he went for a walk. And was lost."

The lines scan for pockets, gestures, traps, the stains and midden-heaps that lives leave behind. Pieces of ash and torn paper occupy the eye while the mind dwells in offices where "information hangs like smoke, copying itself, slowly filling rooms." There is a faith that the world might be reconstructed from the smallest and least significant detail—"A few shells on the table / fragile as 78s"—and that without such details, such evidence of "meagerness," there is nothing to be signified.

Finally, the language—this intimately recognizable vocabulary with which *The Floor and the Breath* is constructed—is its own story, the story of a consciousness in continuous movement, finding in its own oscillations a mirror of the world's. That is the dance whose antithesis is an unthinkable extinction, as he suggests in his poem on the death of Thelonious Monk: "Who ever thinks the syntax will stop / the potlatch of the intelligence be dispersed." The fact of being alive—that ultimate meagerness—sets the measure here. Readers wearied enough of theories and fashions may find its bare and lucid atmosphere bracing to the synapses.

Or, as Michael O'Brien remarks so aptly of the Japanese tanka poets: "The poem doesn't have to go anywhere. If it's any good, it's already there."

Whitman's Revolution

Like Lincoln or Jesus (to both of whom he addressed poems), Walt Whitman has entered irrevocably the realm of myth. In his case the myth is to an astonishing degree of his own design, consciously crafted and deliberately planted. Consider this description of his work from 1867, anticipating in its titanic scale so much subsequent writing about Whitman:

> The idea . . . which is this man's highest contribution, and which, compared even with the vastness of Biblical & Homeric poetry, still looms & towers—as, athwart his fellow-giants of the Himalayas, the dim head of Kunchainjunga rises over the rest—is the idea of Totality. . . . He holds the solution of each & every problem—the spell, giving full satisfaction; and his talisman is *Ensemble.*

This was written, of course, by Whitman himself (under the cover of anonymity) to help publicize an English edition of his poetry. His audacity in raising his own work to the level of the Bible and Homer is matched only by his prescience in gauging accurately his work's future status. He knows how good he is: and if he advertises himself with the expertise of a practiced newspaperman, the gesture is neither cynical nor deluded.

The hyperbolic tone of Whitman's press release has been echoed a thousand times over by poets from Fernando Pessoa ("Entryway to everything! / Bridge to everything! / Highway to everything!") to Hart Crane ("O Saunterer on free ways still

---

Review of *Walt Whitman's America: A Cultural Biography* by David S. Reynolds (New York: Alfred A. Knopf, 1995). Reprinted from *New York Review of Books,* October 19, 1995.

ahead!") to Allen Ginsberg ("dear father, graybeard, lonely old courage-teacher"), from Lorca (who envisioned Whitman with his beard full of butterflies *por el East River y el Bronx*) to the German expressionists Arthur Holitscher ("this floodwave from nature deluging civilization, this veritable tornado of a human being") and Arthur Drey ("Swinger of the torch! Blazing titan of virgin primeval forest!"). When modern poetry has been tempted to fill in for a lost religion, Whitman has most often been called into service as its not altogether reluctant messiah. (His qualms and qualifications with regard to such a role are a constant element of that dialogue with himself in which he ceaselessly revises and parenthetically interprets his own writing.)

A large volume, many large volumes, could be made from such responses, and a collection of the poems dedicated to or inspired by Whitman would encompass the work of Edwin Arlington Robinson, Edgar Lee Masters, Ezra Pound, Carl Sandburg, Vladimir Mayakovsky, Pablo Neruda, Langston Hughes, and Frank O'Hara, not to mention countless high school students, drug users, socially conscious hacks, and government-sponsored apparatchik bards. He is everywhere, often where least expected: Thomas Mann, for instance, weaves an unattributed chunk of "I Sing the Body Electric" (translated into French for good measure) into Hans Castorp's rhapsodic love letter in *The Magic Mountain*. And that singer of Wallace Stevens who "sang beyond the genius of the sea," had she not heard Whitman's "soprano at intervals sailing buoyantly over the tops of immense waves"?

"Be it as if I were with you," he counsels the future reader of his poems. He is and has been with us, so much that we run the risk of mistaking his echo for his voice, and of hearing even in his own lines not so much Whitman as the Whitmanesque. After all, he stated the case modestly when he wrote, "I have offer'd my style to every one." It isn't hard to see him as the inventor, in one passage or another, of free verse, impressionism, imagism, expressionism, surrealism, objectivism, projectivism, open field composition, deep image poetry, and every ramshackle variety of postmodern juxtaposition—and, in another mode, of every modern type of revolutionary anthem, statist ode, and New Age rhapsody.

The successive stylistic tendencies that can be seen as emanating from Whitman—from the rolling grandiosities of early emulators like James Oppenheim and Arturo Giovannitti (not to mention Kahlil Gibran), through the "no ideas but in things" poetic of William Carlos Williams and the street-level notation of Charles Reznikoff, to the resurgence of the long and frankly ecstatic line in Allen Ginsberg and others—have continually found and adapted to their own purposes previously undiscerned qualities of Whitman's poetry.

The episode is not over; we cannot yet look back at the Age of Whitman as a closed chapter. There are tones and textures in him that await their imitators. He has served as an immense quarry of moods and gestures from which poets have chipped away portions of rock, smoothed them, and cut them to more manageable size; or as a sort of cosmic Bettmann Archive whose image bank has been looted to fit the requirements of one program or another, without yet exhausting its holdings. Just as Whitman kept revising his poems throughout his life, changing names and orders and vocabularies, his texts continue to reveal different aspects of themselves in the changing light of history. This is true of any text, but in Whitman's case there is a unique sense that these shifting facets are part of the secret plan, part of the mythical Totality that he adopted as his impossible standard.

He has been with us so much that we need to avoid being suffocated by his myth. One way of evading that hagiographical weight would be to read *Leaves of Grass* as if somebody else had written it. Imagine that, as with Pessoa splintering himself into his "heteronyms," or Valéry Larbaud creating the collected works of his alter ego A. O. Barnabooth, *Leaves of Grass* was intended as a novel in verse, to be read not as self-expression but as detached portraiture of a fictional character. The novel's hero, an eccentric and voluble protagonist who shuttles back and forth between the rural paradise of Long Island and the urban maze of Manhattan, is peculiarly disposed to assume the characteristics of every person and every thing he observes, with sometimes fantastic and sometimes comical results.

He might be a Quixote of the capitalist age, taking literally and with absolute seriousness the spiritual and democratic doctrines mouthed purely for form by established churches and politicians. The novel's secret strategy is to enlist the reader's sympathy for this improbable character, so that in the end it is the world he inhabits that appears out of step.

Reading *Leaves of Grass* that way, we wouldn't need to worry about what Walt really did, or really thought; wouldn't need to determine which experiences he really had and which were imagined, to trace the identities of the amative camerados slipping off into the shadows between the lines of "Calamus," or to probe the motives behind Whitman's multiple denials and fabrications and self-promotions. The unreal reality of Whitman's New York could then be accepted on its own terms, as we accept those other dream cities, Dickens's London and Balzac's Paris.

Indeed, if he had not become himself, Whitman might well have turned out to be one of those extravagantly prolific hacks to whom we owe the adventures of Nick Carter or the Hardy Boys. Fifteen years before *Leaves of Grass,* as a discontented schoolteacher on Long Island, we find him writing to a friend in a parody of popular romance:

> Thank the pitying fates! in two weeks more I shall wind up my affairs, and with tears in my eyes bid a sorrowful adieu to these hallowed precincts.—Shady walks, venerable old school-house, dismantled farms, innocent young ideas—all—all—will I look upon for the last time.—But I must stop—I cannot carry out the affecting thought any farther.—My heart swells, and my melting soul almost expires with the agonizing idea.

The tone is not much different from the wretched fiction he was then grinding out in an attempt at making a living as an author: stories (including the temperance novel *Franklin Evans*) about assorted reprobates, sadists, and doomed waifs, in a style that blends the maudlin and the blood-and-thunder with an occasional blast of the jocular overkill characteristic of nineteenth-century American journalism.

The shadowy margins of *Leaves of Grass* are haunted by the ghosts of Gothic novels he might have written, serials of impossible scope and complexity that might have provided a tour through morgues and back alleys, taverns and brothels, "those places" (as he remarked in an 1864 letter) "where the air is full of the scent of low thievery, druggies, foul play, & prostitution gangrened." In the streets where he was "one of a living crowd" he might well have jostled Poe's solitary and guilt-consumed Man of the Crowd (just as he claimed to have bumped into Poe himself during his early newspaper days in Manhattan):

> Behold through you as bad as the rest,
> Through the laughter, dancing, dining, supping, of people,
> Insides of dresses and ornaments, inside of those wash'd and
> trimm'd faces,
> Behold a secret silent loathing and despair.

The pattern-making of his long poems is easier to relate to the fictional worlds of Dickens or Balzac than to anything that poets were doing in his day. To find the like in poetry it was necessary to go back centuries, to the primal makers he never tired of cataloging:

> The Iliad, Odyssey, plots, doings, wanderings of Eneas,
> Hesiod, Eschylus, Sophocles, Merlin, Arthur,
> The Cid, Roland at Roncesvalles, the Nibelungen . . .

It was always to epic storytellers that he compared himself.

Whitman sets in motion a poetic universe as self-regulating and inherently plausible as Ithaka or Elsinore, and calls it Brooklyn and Manhattan and Long Island. In his extended compositions each line can be seen as a plot-line flung out into space, as if the poem were a string of beginnings: not one novel but a hundred, a catalog of destinies, "all identities that have existed or may exist on this globe, or any globe," as he specifies with almost legalistic thoroughness. As it happened, neither fiction nor verse as they then existed could provide Whitman with what he needed, so he invented out of necessity his own form, a reversion to what he conceived of as the most archaic bardic impulses, representing itself as the poetry of the future.

To look for biographical realities in *Leaves of Grass* is to read Whitman as he does not want to be read. Even he, he insists, knows of his own life only "a few hints, a few diffused faint clews and indirections" that he seeks "for my own use to trace here": his own use, not anyone else's. He had every reason to surmise how little a biography could tell about him, especially since he had helped to obscure matters by planting innumerable apocryphal details in his writings and conversation. It remains astonishing that a life so well documented—in letters, photographs, press clippings, and detailed memoirs such as his disciple Horace Traubel's three-volume *With Walt Whitman in Camden*—should nevertheless elude close inspection. Rumor and speculation take over rather swiftly when one goes beyond the surface of Whitman's life, beyond the succession of images he vetted for public consumption. Cryptic entries in notebooks and letters, patterns of emendation and rearrangement in poetic texts: it is to such evidence that scholars resort to learn fundamental things about this ostensibly frankest and most self-revealing of poets.

He does not make it easy for them. There is barely an autobiographical statement of Whitman's that has not been challenged, from that early encounter with Poe to his alleged early years of wandering across America, now reduced by investigators to a mere three months in New Orleans (that "populous city" with its "woman who passionately clung to me," a woman who was the Dark Lady for Whitmanites until she turned out, in an earlier draft, to have been a man). Like a rock star supervising his own publicity, he retained control over nearly every intimate glimpse we get of him. We are not permitted to know everything and, what's more, he assures us that we don't want to know: "O admirers, praise not me—compliment not me—you make me wince, / I see what you do not—I know what you do not."

In his biography *Walt Whitman's America,* David S. Reynolds enlists the whole American scene of Whitman's time to explain him—if anything can explain him. Reynolds underestimates, I think, the extent to which we need Whitman to explain America, but that is a question that does not really enter into his study, which amounts to a systematic and superbly researched work of annotation. If for many contemporary readers Whitman's poetry seems to float beyond its own time, Reynolds lays out how thoroughly it draws on the materials of its moment: the vocabulary and gestures of phrenology and popular physiology, trance poems and animal magnetism, socialism and free love, Free Soilers and Loco Focos, orators, history painters, opera singers, Shakespearean actors, cheapjack illuminati like Thomas Lake Harris and Andrew Jackson Davis, the Poughkeepsie Seer. No solitary singer, this is a Whitman steeped in the entertainments, fads, and debates of his time, newshound and partisan.

As an evocation of America, and above all of New York, in the antebellum era, Reynolds' book teems with the cacophonous and frequently anarchic energies of a culture in which, we are told, "by 1843 there were between twenty and thirty thousand mesmerists lecturing in the Northeast alone," in which the great tragedian Junius Brutus Booth "walked the streets as Shylock or Richard, flinging coins to people who paraded after him," in which (in Whitman's enumeration) "free-lovers, ultra-abolitionists, trance-media, female atheists, vegetarians, phrenologists" gathered in the thousands for an 1858 convention in Rutland, Vermont.

The motley nature of Whitman's intellectual and aesthetic influences couldn't be more appropriate to his democratic poetic. He found sustenance at every hand, in material now entirely obscure, such as Fanny Wright's 1822 radical deist novel *Ten Days in Athens* ("I kept it about me for years"), John Howard Payne's drama *Brutus, or the Fall of Tarquin* ("affected me for weeks . . . permanently filter'd into my whole nature"), genre paintings like those of the Long Island artist William Sidney Mount, the harmonizing of the Hutchinson family singers (whose most popular song was openly autobiographical and incorporated their own names—a song of themselves), and the eccentric verse of McDonald Clarke, the Mad Poet of Broadway, whom Whitman felt "possessed all the requisites of a great poet," and who died in jail after being picked up for vagrancy in 1842. In short, Walt's barbaric yawp was far from an isolated noise in an otherwise genteel society. Reynolds finds much precedent for Whitman's poetic innovations in a street culture valuing public performance with full audience participation; the exuberant mingling of high-flown and vulgar styles; the unrestrained venting of emotional extremes whether in the pulpit, on stage, or on the political platform.

Two city types were of particular importance for Whitman:

the b'hoys of the Bowery (the proletarian playgoers and volunteer firemen whom he characterized as "splendid and rugged") and the "roughs, rowdies, or loafers," described by Reynolds as "a distinct class of gang members and street loungers who roved through Manhattan's poorer districts and often instigated riots." Reynolds argues convincingly that Whitman's persona in the first *Leaves of Grass* of 1855—"wicked rather than conventionally virtuous, free, smart, prone to slang and vigorous outbursts"—is imbued with the manners of these subcultures. When he labels himself "one of the roughs," when he "leans and loafs" at his ease, Whitman is evoking an immediately recognizable cluster of traits and associations, so that it was no gratuitous slam for a contemporary reviewer to describe him as "the 'Bowery Bhoy' in literature."

But Whitman was not, Reynolds suggests, merely celebrating this pugnacious and heterogeneous urban culture. He was cleansing it of impurities, offering it up in an idealized form designed to spark self-improvement in the popular audience he sought by channeling their rough energies into higher forms. Taking in the poison bred by human greed and desire, he filters it through himself and transforms it into beauty, just as (in "This Compost") the earth transmutes human corpses into the purity of nature:

> Now I am terrified at the Earth, it is that calm and patient,
> It grows such sweet things out of such corruptions,
> It turns harmless and stainless on its axis, with such endless
> successions of diseas'd corpses,
> It distills such exquisite winds out of such infused fetor.

The quest for purification accords with the reformers and sex theorists of the day, countering degeneracy and sexual license with sound heredity and a healthy virility. Sex as propounded in the "Children of Adam" poems is more healthful than erotic, and the passages where Whitman evokes masturbation, however revolutionary in their frankness, are far from approving: "Have you seen the fool that corrupted his own live body? or the fool that corrupted her own live body? / For they do not conceal themselves, and cannot conceal themselves."

Reynolds pays particular attention to Orson Fowler (of Fowlers and Wells, the publishers of the 1855 *Leaves of Grass*), author of *Love and Parentage* and *Sexual Science;* in such publications can be found the roots, for instance, of Whitman's physiological catalogs—"Leg-fibres, knee, knee-pan, upper-leg, under-leg"—with their scientific rather than voluptuous tone. So far were those poems from being extemporaneous outpourings that Whitman prepared for them with methodical research, as evidenced in a notebook entry: "Read the latest and best anatomical works/talk with physicians/study the anatomical plates."

Here as elsewhere Reynolds's point is that to read Whitman without knowing where his vocabulary comes from (whether the terms in question are phrenological or Swedenborgian), and without knowing the contemporary debates into which he interjects himself, is to read him in a vacuum in which it becomes much easier to recast him in whatever idealized form the reader favors.

The question of how Whitman's contemporaries construed him (when they read him at all) enters into an interesting discussion by Reynolds of the "Calamus" poems, whose homoeroticism was less shocking in Whitman's day than later generations have supposed: "Passionate intimacy between people of the same sex was common in pre-Civil War America. . . . Whatever the nature of his physical relationships with [men], most of the passages about same-sex love in his poems were not out of keeping with then-current theories and practices that underscored the healthiness of such love." It was in fact the explicitness of the dutifully heterosexual "Children of Adam" poems that caused most of the trouble for Whitman in the nineteenth century.

The world that shaped Whitman was in a state of upheaval that took his family from a sedentary rural way of life into all the disasters of rapid expansion and ruthless market economics. The farmland of his childhood—the terrain that his nostalgia transforms into terrestrial paradise—turned rapidly into congested urban space. The population of Brooklyn went from four thousand to more than two hundred thousand between 1810 and

1855, even though the resulting surge in construction work failed to rescue Whitman's carpenter father from financial failure.

Whitman's origins are mysterious in their very ordinariness, and what little he has to say about his early family life is usually cloaked in nostalgia. His father turns up unmistakably and indelibly in *Leaves of Grass*—"The father, strong, selfsufficient, manly, mean, angered, unjust, / The blow, the quick loud word, the tight bargain, the crafty lure,"—and his intellectual legacy to his son included the political radicalism of Tom Paine and the Quaker spirituality of Elias Hicks; but after his death Whitman barely mentioned him again.

His mother he remained close to all her life, and by his own account never really got over her death in 1873. In the heartbreakingly simple and direct letters he wrote to her during his hospital service in the Civil War ("& then the agony I see every day, I get almost frightened at the world—Mother, I will try to write more cheerfully next time—but I see so much—") it is difficult to tell who leaned more on the other for consolation. Surviving portraits of Whitman's parents—eroded faces, haunted eyes—speak of a suffering that has beaten them down to anger or resignation. Looking at them, it is hard not to recall Whitman's many pronouncements on photography and the expressive power of faces. Perhaps his many photographic portraits, calculated to convey a serene wisdom, were a deliberate reply to these stark daguerreotypes.

Out of his seven siblings, one died in a madhouse, one drank himself to death at an early age, leaving a widow who became a prostitute, one was a possible psychotic whose husband died in a madhouse, and one suffered severe mental and physical handicaps. He went to work early, as printer's apprentice and miserably unhappy schoolteacher; edited a staggering variety of newspapers, rarely for long at a stretch; immersed himself in the vociferous confrontations of Democratic Party politics, and perhaps almost found in politics an alternative to a poetic career; went to the opera and had his bumps read by a phrenologist. He met scores of working-class men and wrote their names in notebooks. Later, talking about the origins of *Leaves of Grass,* he explained that "the book arose out of my life in Brooklyn and

New York from 1838 to 1853, absorbing a million people, for fifteen years, with an intimacy, an eagerness, an abandon, probably never equalled." It's as good an explanation as any of where *Leaves of Grass* came from.

To read Whitman and think about his life is to come back sooner or later to that central mystery. A study of cultural influence such as *Walt Whitman's America* cannot really confront it head-on. As Reynolds turns up more and more sources, the reader may begin to feel as if the making of *Leaves of Grass* were a passive phenomenon, an accretion of what was going on around Whitman. In such an extravagant world—what with the mad actors and their riotous fans, the street gangs in the pay of corrupt politicians, the armed conflicts breaking out over slavery, the bands of inspired mystics and sex-scientists—how could something as absolutely radical and unanticipated as Whitman's poetry *not* have emerged?

Yet although the whole population was subject to the same influences, only one of them was influenced to write "Song of Myself" or anything remotely resembling it. There are singularities beyond the reach of social history. Examining separately all the influences that Whitman may have absorbed—through his constant ground-level attentiveness, his ear for slang and jargon, his capacity for assuming every passing role, his endless expeditions on ferry and bus and pavement—would not enable us, in the absence of his text, to imagine the use he made of them. He once said he couldn't have done it without Italian opera; again, it is as good an explanation as any.

Walt Whitman's America greatly enriches our reading of Whitman without necessarily coming any closer to getting behind his many masks. In the book's later chapters, which trace the gradual diminution of Whitman's poetic energies in the years after the Civil War, his softening of the radicalism of the early poetry, and his tenacious efforts to gain public support for his work, a loss of sympathy on Reynolds's part is apparent. He is evidently not happy about Whitman's writing poems in praise of Custer and Kaiser Friedrich Wilhelm, or about his newfound enthusiasm for the magnates of the Gilded Age, and this leads him to a somewhat severer view of Whitman's motives and conduct that seems warranted. Admittedly, the insufferable aura of religious devotion permeating the circle around Whitman in his last years would be enough to arouse contrariness in any biographer.

Ultimately the question of what influenced Whitman cannot be addressed without admitting how ineluctably he has influenced us. He isn't merely the creature but the creator of his times, which on crucial levels we see through his eyes. A certain circularity sets in: Whitman could exist because of the vitality of his age, his age was vital because it engendered a Whitman. We could hardly know that vitality without him; he tells what no one else would. His poetic testimony is of a different order than the reports of newspapers (including his own); he offers another way into his historical moment, in which we share the sensations of the observer.

This was his democratic literary revolution, in which every figure in the crowd—everyone who in Shakespeare and Scott would have been an anonymous spear-carrier—is endowed as never before with brain and heart and lungs and genitals. He sees them in their bodies, and so makes physical appetite, physical being, part of literature in a way it had rarely been since Rabelais, and with an intent utterly foreign to Rabelais. Here the body is not seen from without, as the subject of grotesque comedy, but experienced from within as the site where a cosmic epic plays itself out. "Behold, the body includes and is the meaning, the main concern, and includes and is the soul."

Not that some echo of Rabelaisian grotesquerie is altogether missing, in a passage like this from "Faces":

> This now is too lamentable a face for a man,
> Some abject louse asking leave to be, cringing for it,
> Some milk-nosed maggot blessing what lets it wrig to its hole,
> This face is a dog's snout sniffing for garbage,
> Snakes nest in that mouth.

Wherever the body is rejected or covered up we find traces of such a morbid farce, swarming with death's-heads and diseased faces worthy of a medieval memento mori—memorials of the old corrupt world, the world of feudal hierarchies and priestly prohibitions. (As for Rabelais, Whitman thought well enough of him to propose him, in collaboration with Michelangelo, Plutarch, and Aeschylus, as an ideal portraitist of Lincoln.)

Something is generally presumed to have happened—a mystical revelation, an erotic revelation, or both at once—to account for the rather sudden transformation of the author of *Franklin Evans* into the author of *Song of Myself*. For Reynolds it is connected as well to the failure of his political ambitions: "In the fifties, his collapsed belief in the party system and presidential power had caused the incredible surge of his omnivorous, all-gathering poetic 'I,' creating his richest poetry." A dissolution of some kind—or of all kinds—must have preceded such a flooding.

But ecstasies and breakdowns were as commonplace then as they are now. Extravagant visionaries abounded, and they frequently wrote long poems to embody their visions. What was crucial for Whitman must have been the realization that—unlike anyone he was aware of in his vicinity—he possessed a literary method adequate to his cosmic impulses. The 1855 *Leaves of Grass* makes clear that he has thought more about poetry, from more angles, in more contexts actual and potential, than anyone around him: and that he knows it.

Along with everything else that it is, the book can be read as a protracted and deliberate work of literary criticism, showing by example every way in which nineteenth-century American poetry failed to make contact with the world in which it existed. "I sometimes think," he remarked years later to Traubel, "the *Leaves* is only a language experiment." It made all the difference to grasp with the utmost clarity that it was words, not ideas or feelings or ineffable aspirations, that were his tools. He can step outside language—"Were you thinking that those were the words, those upright lines? those curves, angles, dots?"—only by having grasped what language is. It is as if he stepped out of a trap.

His genius was above all technical. If we don't quite see that, if we still incline to see in *Leaves of Grass* a species of spontaneous organic utterance rather than a cunning exercise in verbal architecture, it is all the more tribute to his skill as builder. A flow consisting of absolutely separate elements: such is the optical illusion he manufactures, more deeply persuasive than any magic lantern show. "I will not make poems with reference to parts, / But I will make poems, songs, thoughts, with reference to ensemble." He could not have done so without establishing that the poem consists of nothing but parts.

In the notebook poem "Pictures," predating *Leaves of Grass* by a few years, he has already found what he needs. The contents of his mind can be enumerated like pictures on a wall, or more properly like descriptions of pictures in a catalog:

> In a little house pictures I keep, many pictures hanging
> suspended—It is not a fixed house,
> It is round—it is but a few inches from one side of it to the
> other side,
> But behold! it has room enough—in it, hundreds and
> thousands,—all the varieties . . .

The elements are free and independent; they can go anywhere; they can be anywhere. Things can be placed side by side; they can be rearranged; they participate in a totality no matter how jagged the contrasts among them. He can put them wherever he wants them to go.

It is a physical perception, as if Whitman had taken apart what he was given, literally with scissors, and discerned an infinity of uses in the pieces spread out before him, a thousand ways to exercise his henceforth assured sense of balance and decorum: strings of words, juxtapositions of strings of words: "flicker of black contrasted with wild red and yellow light," or "stars, rain, snow, my amaze," or "heard the pulse of you when all was still ringing little bells last night under my ear," or "filament, filament, filament." By so simple a procedure—a matter of carpentry, of mechanics—it becomes possible to sidestep a world of rhetorical and narrative encumberments.

He had the builder's eye for foundations and crossbeams, the professional printer's eye accustomed to the alphabet lying loose in trays. "My theory is that the author might be the maker even of the body of his book—set the type, print the book on a press, put a cover on it, all with his own hands." In the ponderousness of those long lines one can feel him actually hoisting the line into place, laying down one alongside the other, as if the point after all were to appreciate that muscular heave. He has the calm assurance of a builder whose blueprint is thoroughly in order: to a remarkable degree Whitman's program for his poetry *is* his poetry. He makes a list of things to do and by that very act they are done; by describing the poem of the future, as if in an exhibition catalog, he brings it into being.

It is a job of work: "I had great trouble in leaving out the stock 'poetical' touches, but succeeded at last," as if it had been a matter of scraping off barnacles or accretions of rust. No nonsense, no question of angelic inspiration. If he works with preternatural energy, it is because he is fired up with the awareness of his unique and solitary opportunity. He has no trouble keeping in mind the theme of his work, because the theme is nothing other than himself working on it. *Leaves of Grass* is a description of what it is like to be writing *Leaves of Grass.*

The process never ended. The poems were made of pieces, item by item; and then remade, given new names, the parts shifted around, the poems made parts of larger clusters. Whitman's parenthetical comments on his own writing—fleeting self-contradictions, winks, changes of emphasis—become part of the poem. Aside from professional scholars, few readers of Whitman have even begun to read the major editions of *Leaves of Grass,* with their drastic shifts in arrangement and continual revision, as separate and very different works.

Few remarks of Whitman's have been so widely quoted as the disclaimer in his late essay "A Backward Glance o'er Travel'd Roads": "No one will get at my verses who insists upon viewing them as a literary performance, or attempt at such performance, or as aiming mainly toward art or aestheticism." Given the kind of aesthetic analysis he might have expected to receive in his own day, the statement is understandable enough, but its absolutism is undercut by Whitman's own repeated acknowledgment of his aesthetic motivation, what he once called his "artism." If these acknowledgments are somewhat marginal, that is in accord with the "curious removes" and "indirections" proper to "the poet, the esthetic worker in any field." The triumphant openness of *Leaves* has as its obverse a ubiquitous concealment: it is a kind of open-air labyrinth, or like the web of that "noiseless patient spider" with whom he identified himself. "There is something *furtive* in my nature," he told a friend, "like an old hen." What he had given himself in *Leaves* was a field large enough in which to hide anything, any desire.

Nothing is hidden, however, from the reader for whom he longs, the reader one is invited to become, the reader whose tongue is in Whitman's mouth—"It is you talking just as much as myself, I act as the tongue of you"—and who looks out of Whitman's eyes: "Just as you feel when you look on the river and sky, so I felt." For what purpose, after all, was all this created if not to provide a space in which Whitman and his reader could be alone together?

By force of will he perpetuates not only himself but a world for him and his comrade to inhabit, a world made from the vital stuff around him but reordered to his specifications. The life of the reader is all that is needful to make it live:

> I that was visible am become invisible,
> Now it is you, compact, visible, realizing my poems, seeking me,
> Fancying how happy you were if I could be with you and
>   become your comrade;
> Be it as if I were with you. (Be not too certain but I am now with
>   you.)

He has found a way to keep himself alive through those generations of future readers in whom he hopes "to arouse and set flowing . . . endless streams of living, pulsating love and friendship, directly from them to myself, now and ever." All he asks from the reader, then, is eternal and unconditional love. An incalculable number have found the exchange quite reasonable.

UNDER DISCUSSION

David Lehman, General Editor
Donald Hall, Founding Editor

Volumes in the Under Discussion series collect reviews and essays about individual poets. The series is concerned with contemporary American and English poets about whom the consensus has not yet been formed and the final vote has not been taken. Titles in the series include:

Charles Simic
edited by Bruce Weigl
On Gwendolyn Brooks
edited by Stephen Caldwell Wright
On William Stafford
edited by Tom Andrews
Denise Levertov
edited with an introduction by Albert Gelpi
The Poetry of W. D. Snodgrass
edited by Stephen Haven
On the Poetry of Philip Levine
edited by Christopher Buckley
Frank O'Hara
edited by Jim Elledge
James Wright
edited by Peter Stitt and Frank Graziano
Anne Sexton
edited by Steven E. Colburn
On Louis Simpson
edited by Hank Lazer
On the Poetry of Galway Kinnell
edited by Howard Nelson
Robert Creeley's Life and Work
edited by John Wilson
Robert Bly: When Sleepers Awake
edited by Joyce Peseroff
On the Poetry of Allen Ginsberg
edited by Lewis Hyde
Reading Adrienne Rich
edited by Jane Roberta Cooper
Richard Wilbur's Creation
edited and with an introduction by Wendy Salinger
Elizabeth Bishop and Her Art
edited by Lloyd Schwartz and Sybil P. Estess